birds of pray

margaret weber

birds of pray

mixed media works

2010 - 2014

Margaret Weber
BIRDS OF PRAY

Book design : Loura van der Meule and Emily de Rham
Photography : Edward Fausty

Printed and bound in the United States of America.
ISBN-13: 978-1539196006
ISBN-10: 1539196003

BIRDS OF PRAY is also available in an 11" x 13" hard cover edition.
Contact Margaret Weber : webmargar@gmail.com

VICTORY HALL, INC., composed of **VICTORY HALL PRESS**, Drawing Rooms, and Rainbow Thursdays, is a not-for-profit arts organization based in the NJ/NY metro area. It is directed by James Pustorino and funded in part by the New Jersey State Council on the Arts/Department of State, a partner agency of the National Endowment for the Arts, administered by the Hudson County Office of Cultural and Heritage Affairs, Thomas A. Degise, County Executive, and the Board of Chosen Freeholders.
Contact : victoryhall1@msn.com
Website : victoryhall.org

For Zoe

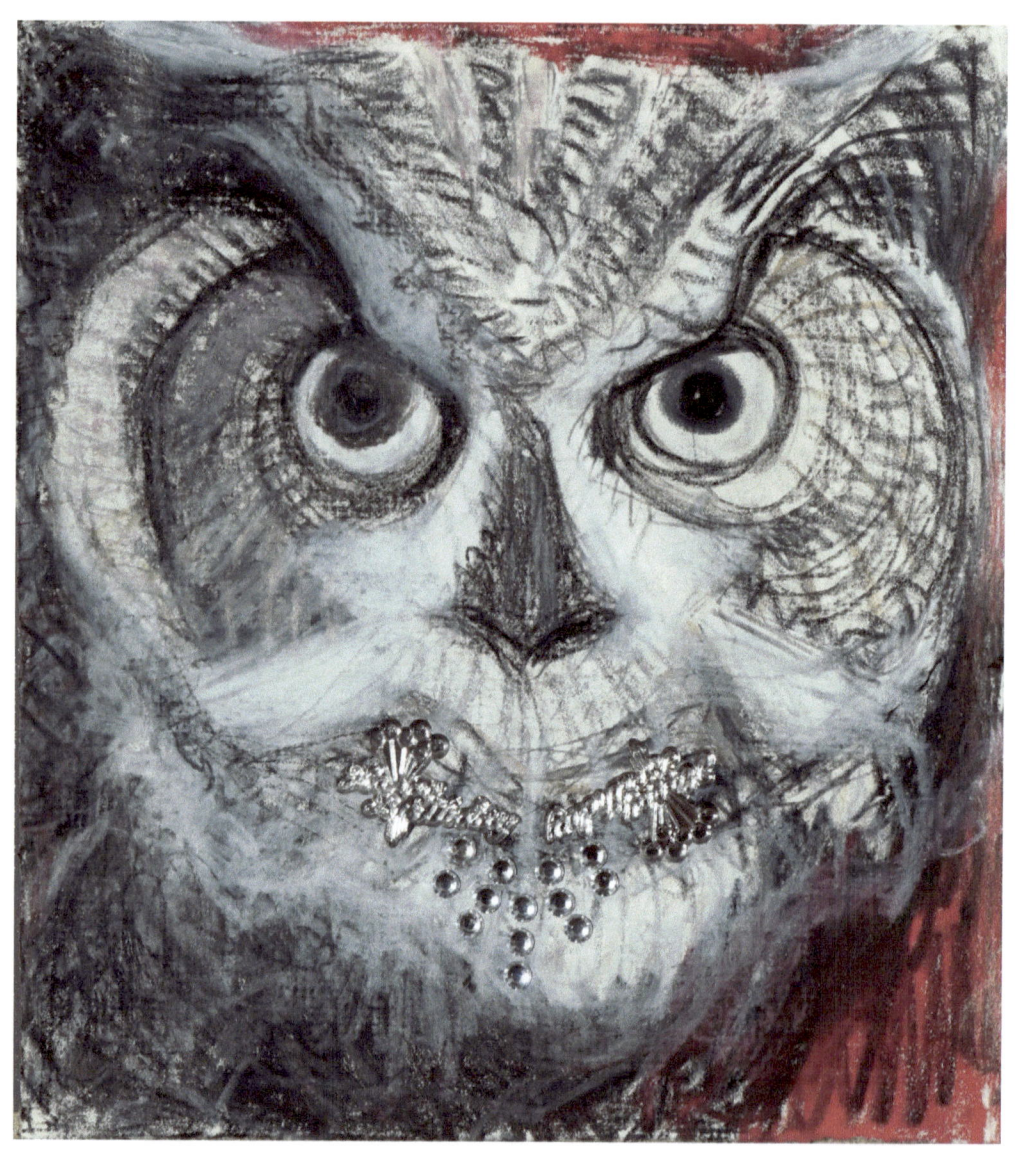

I

I intend my work to nestle in the space between beautiful and ugly,

to dance between mundane and sacred, to jostle between OK and WTF!

The birds are embodiments of the threatened world of nature

and a spiritual aspect or projection of humans,

an alter ego, in a sense: knowing and vulnerable.

Textiles, which are an element in many of these images, have played a

continuing role in human history since prehistoric times.

Incorporation of design into woven material worn by early humans

shows the extraordinary importance which marks of color and shape had for them.

These works help me explore a connection to, and fear for, nature and

a sense that I am part of a continuum of human endeavor.

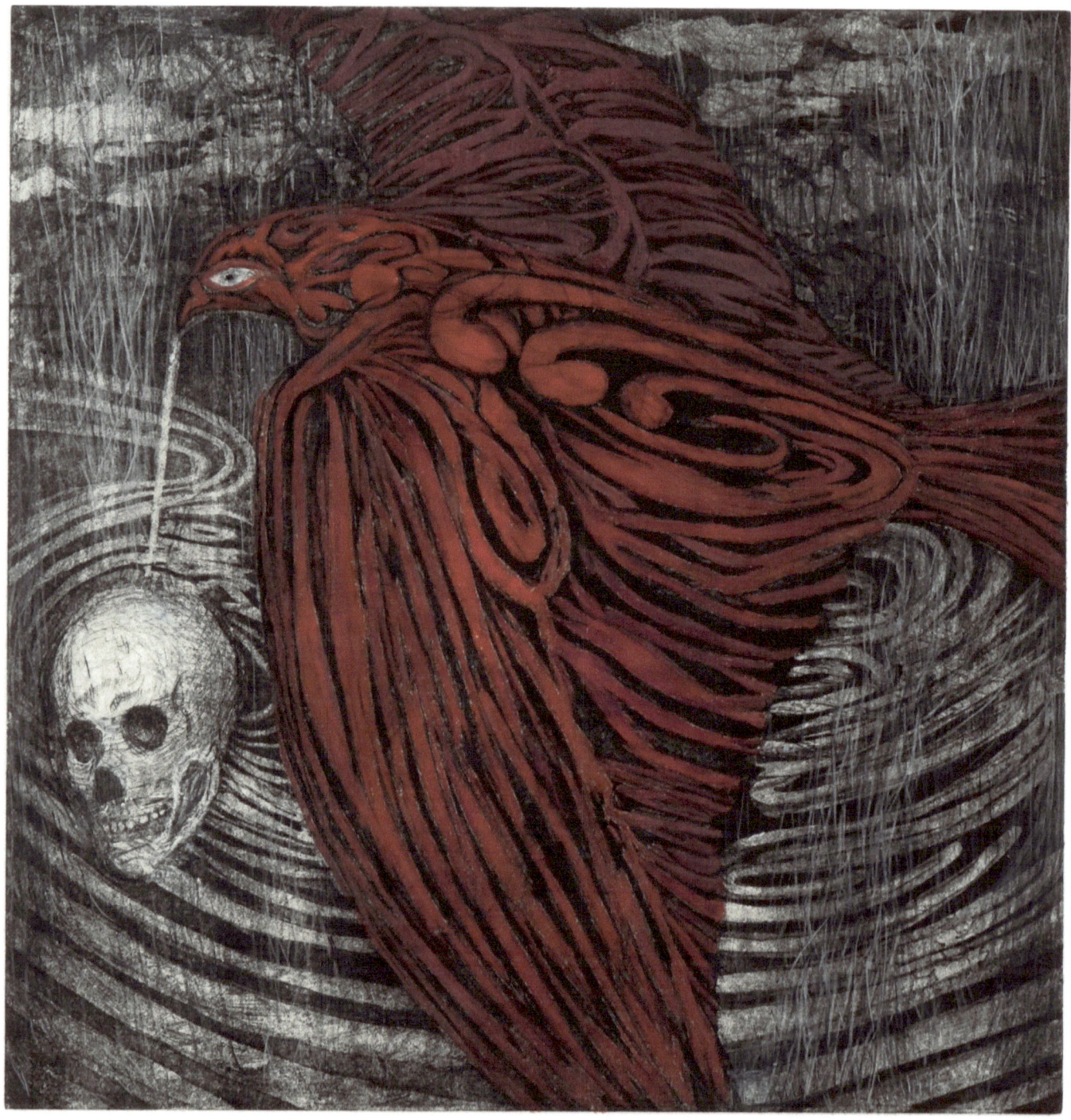

3

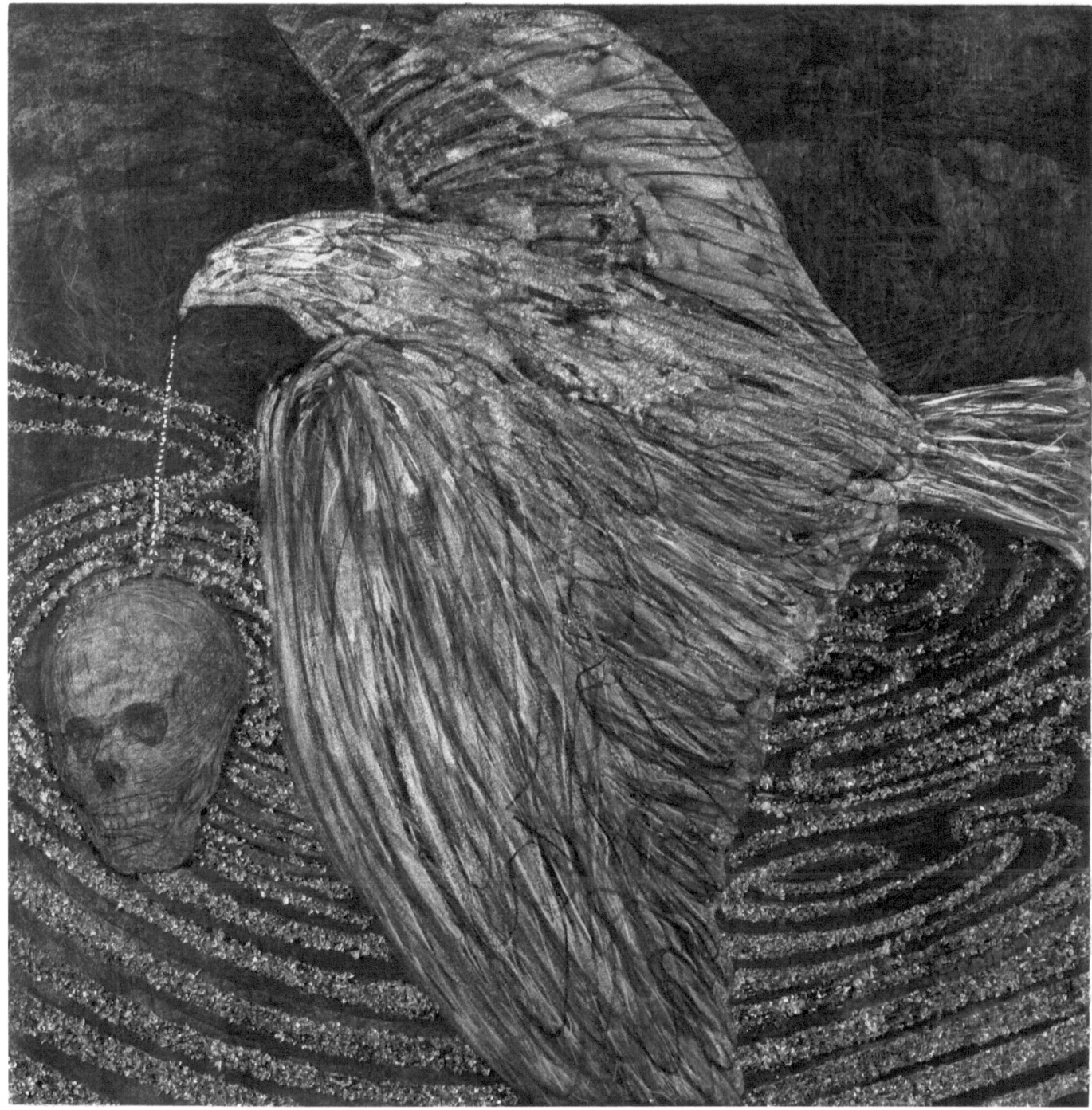

4

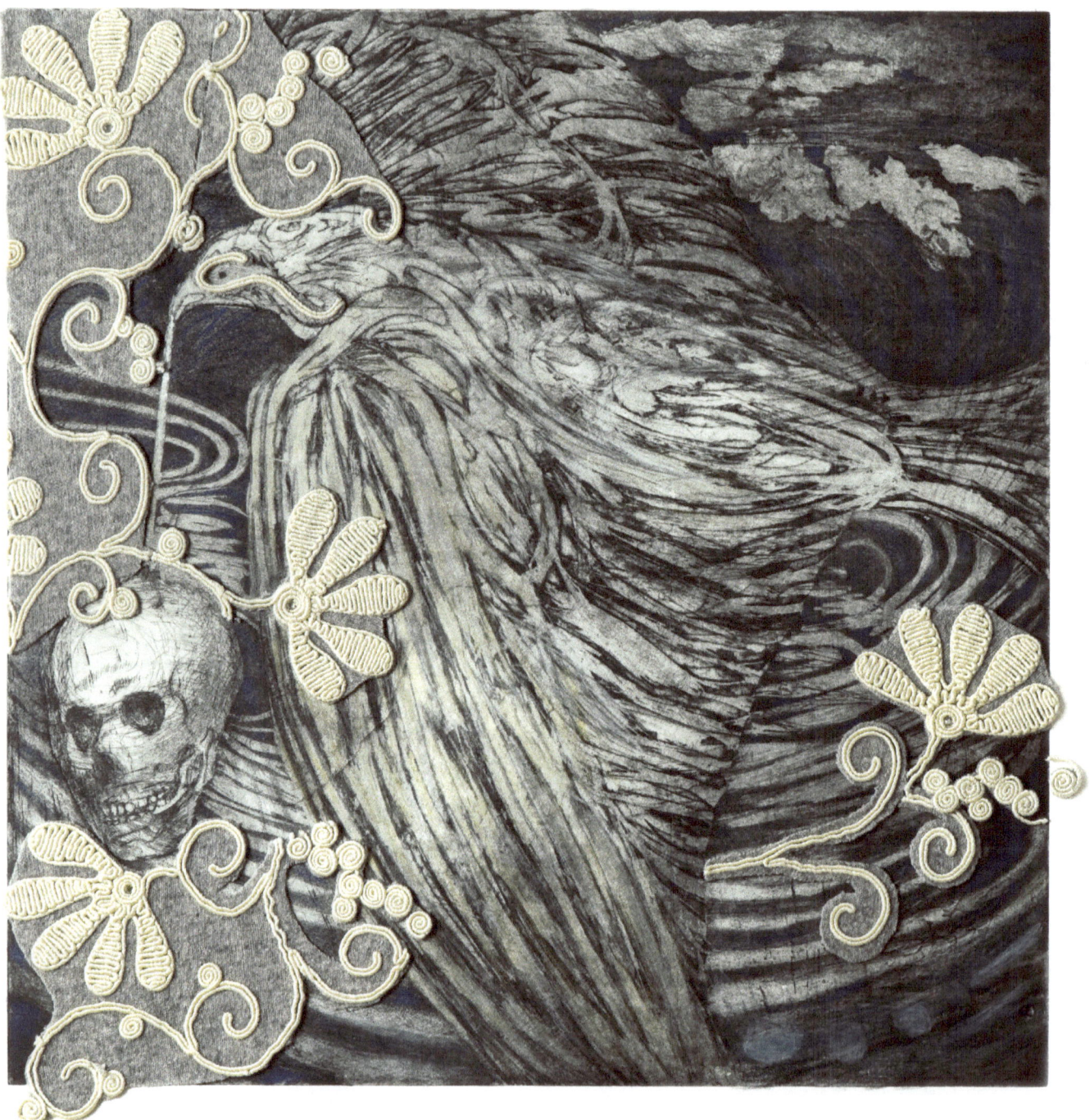

5

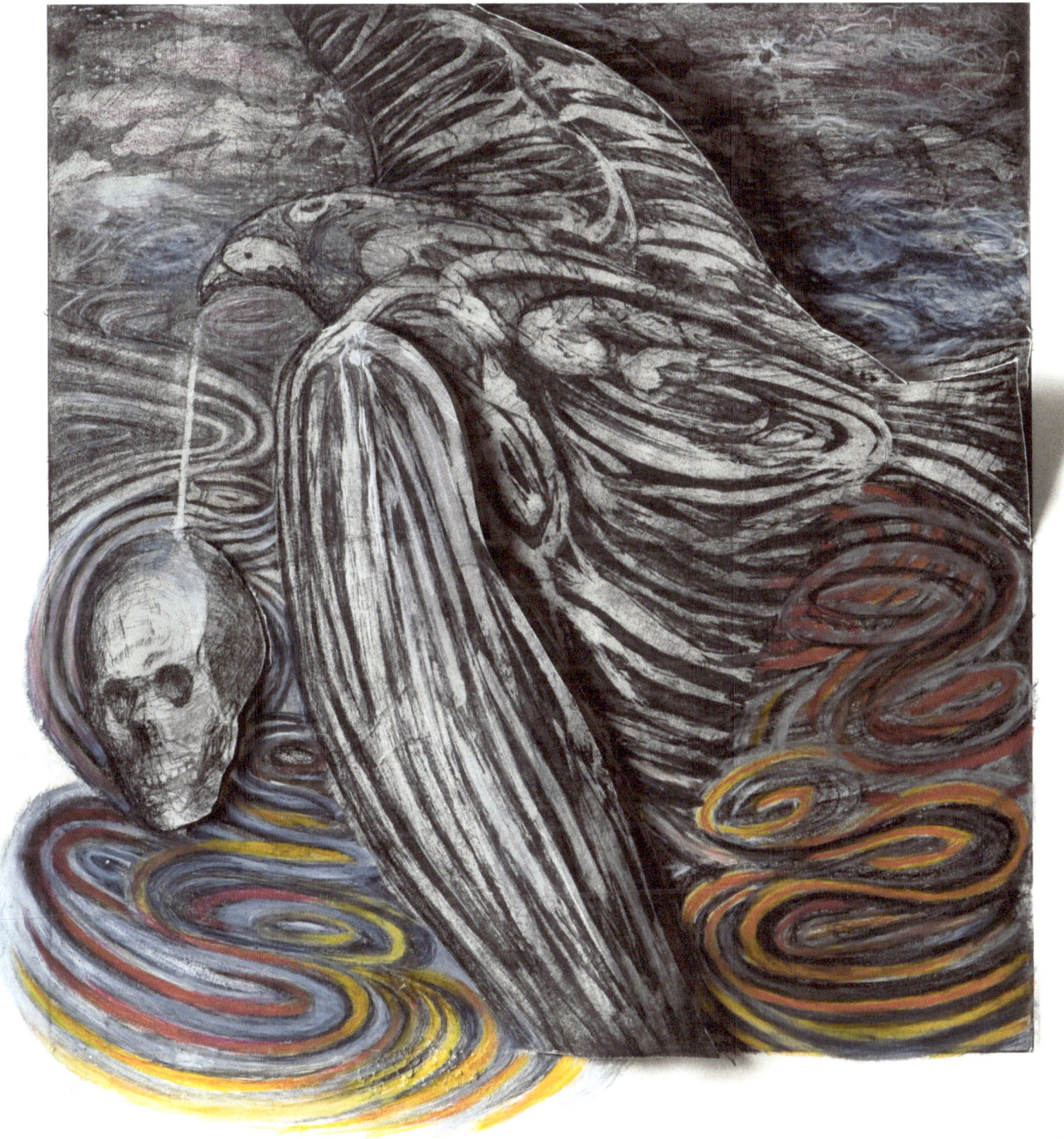

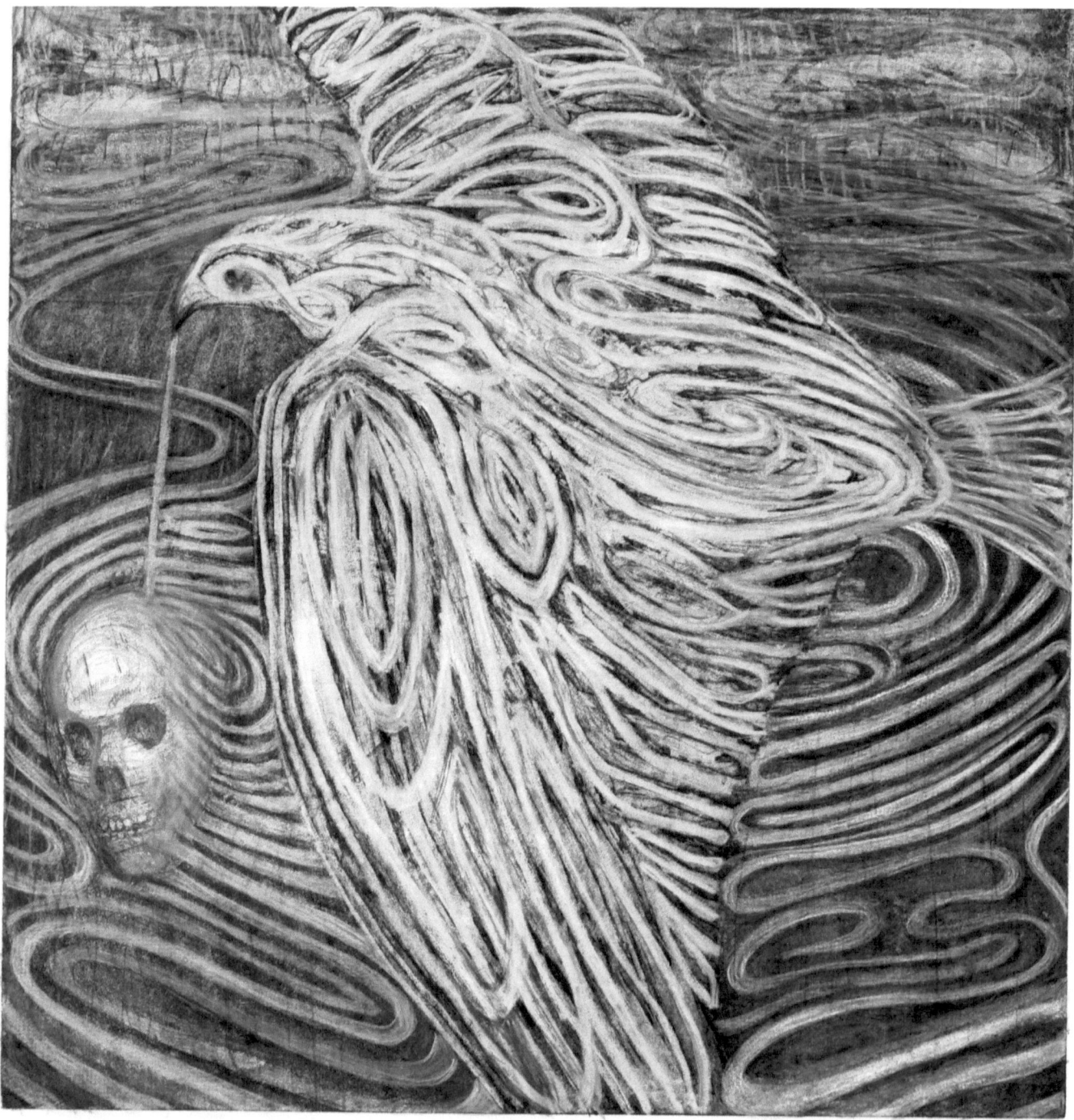

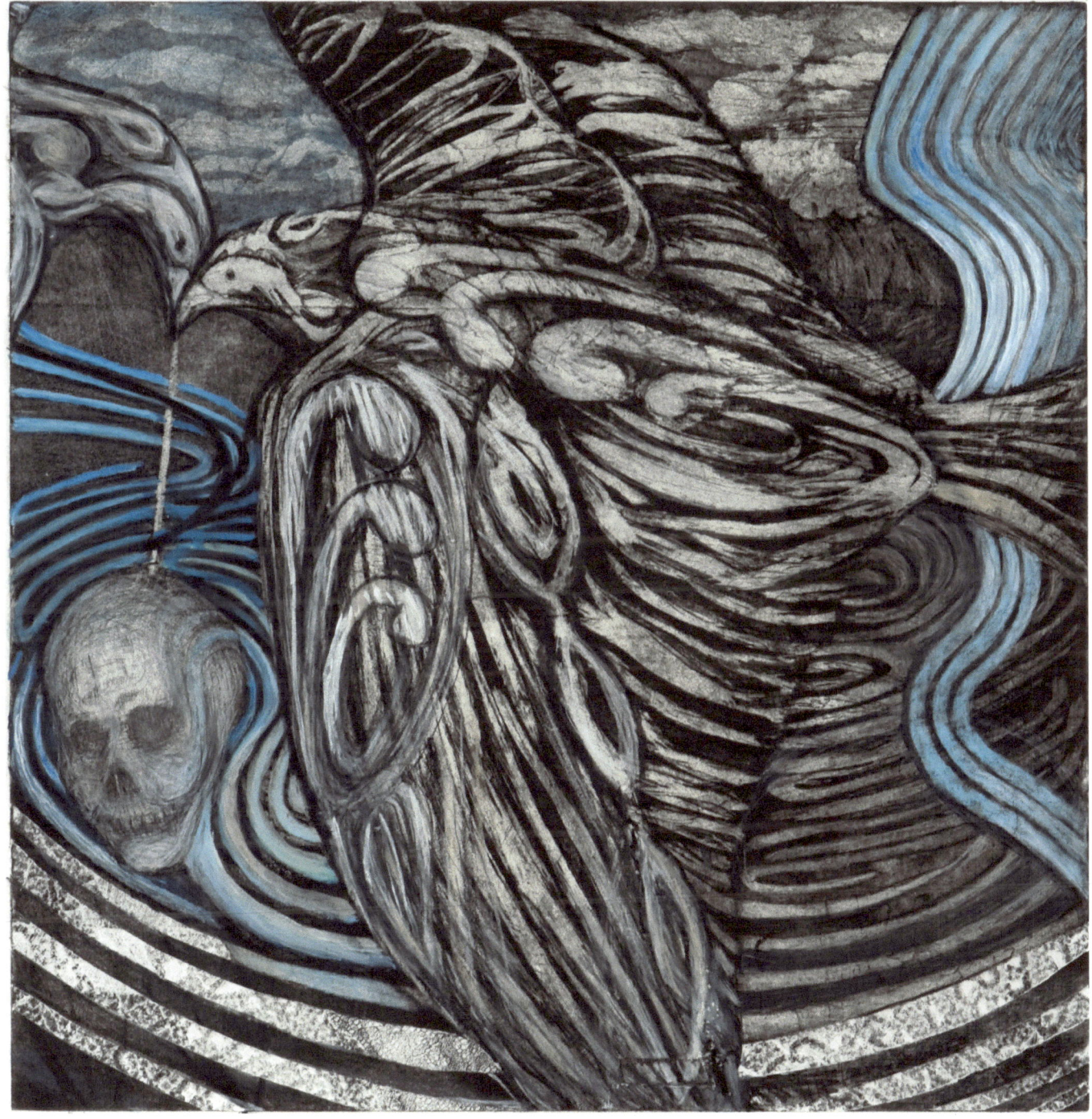

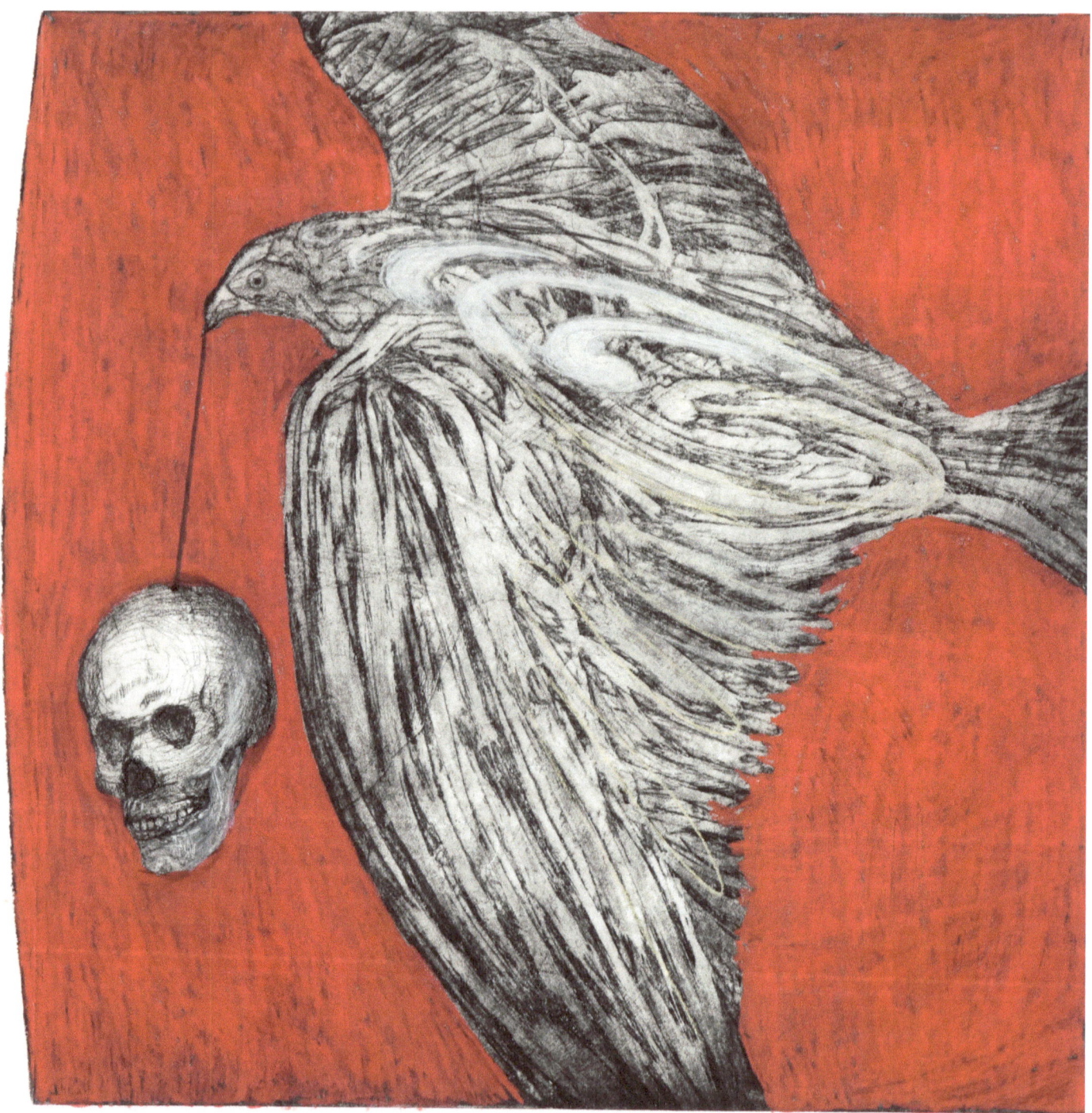

9

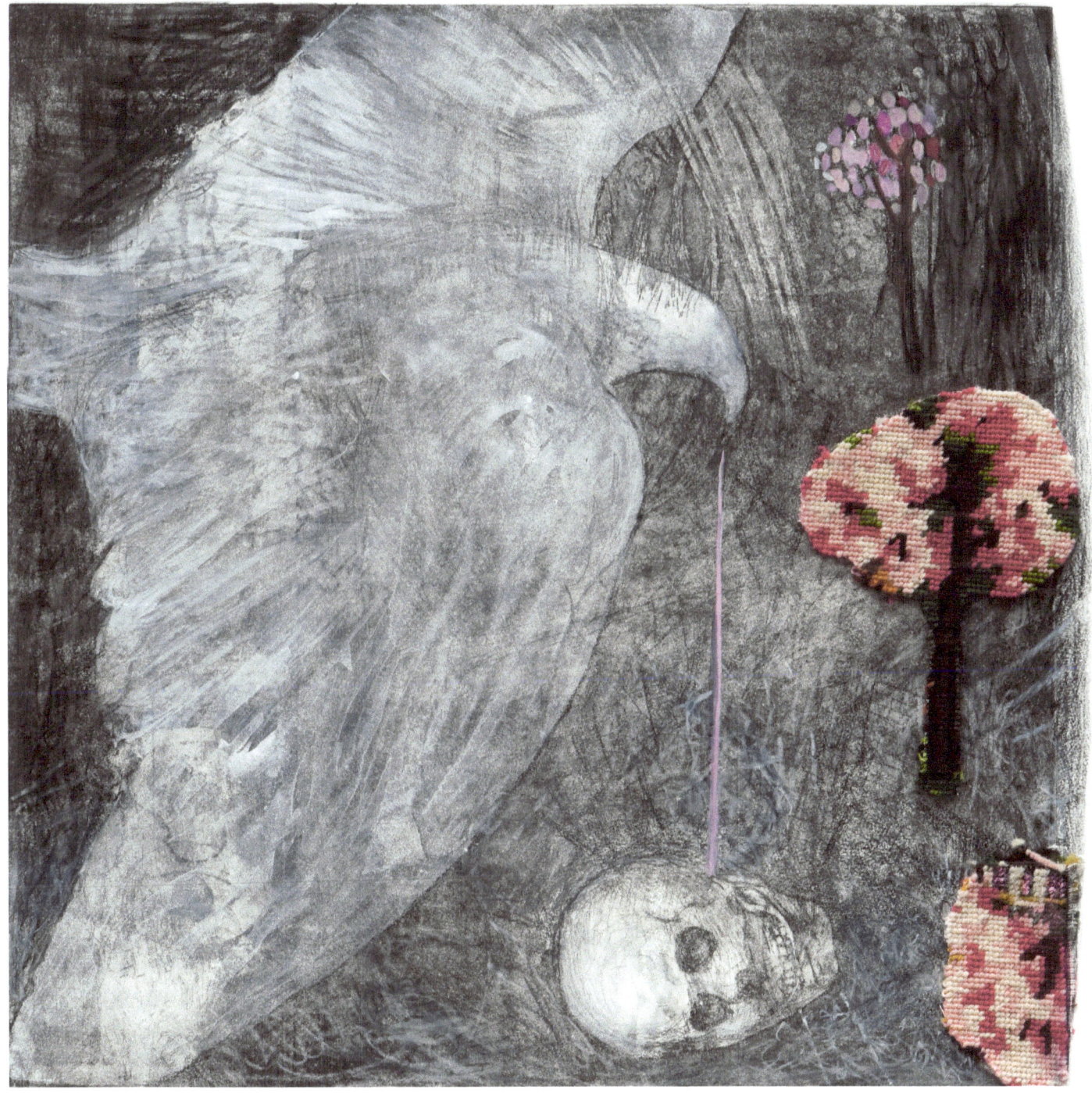

10

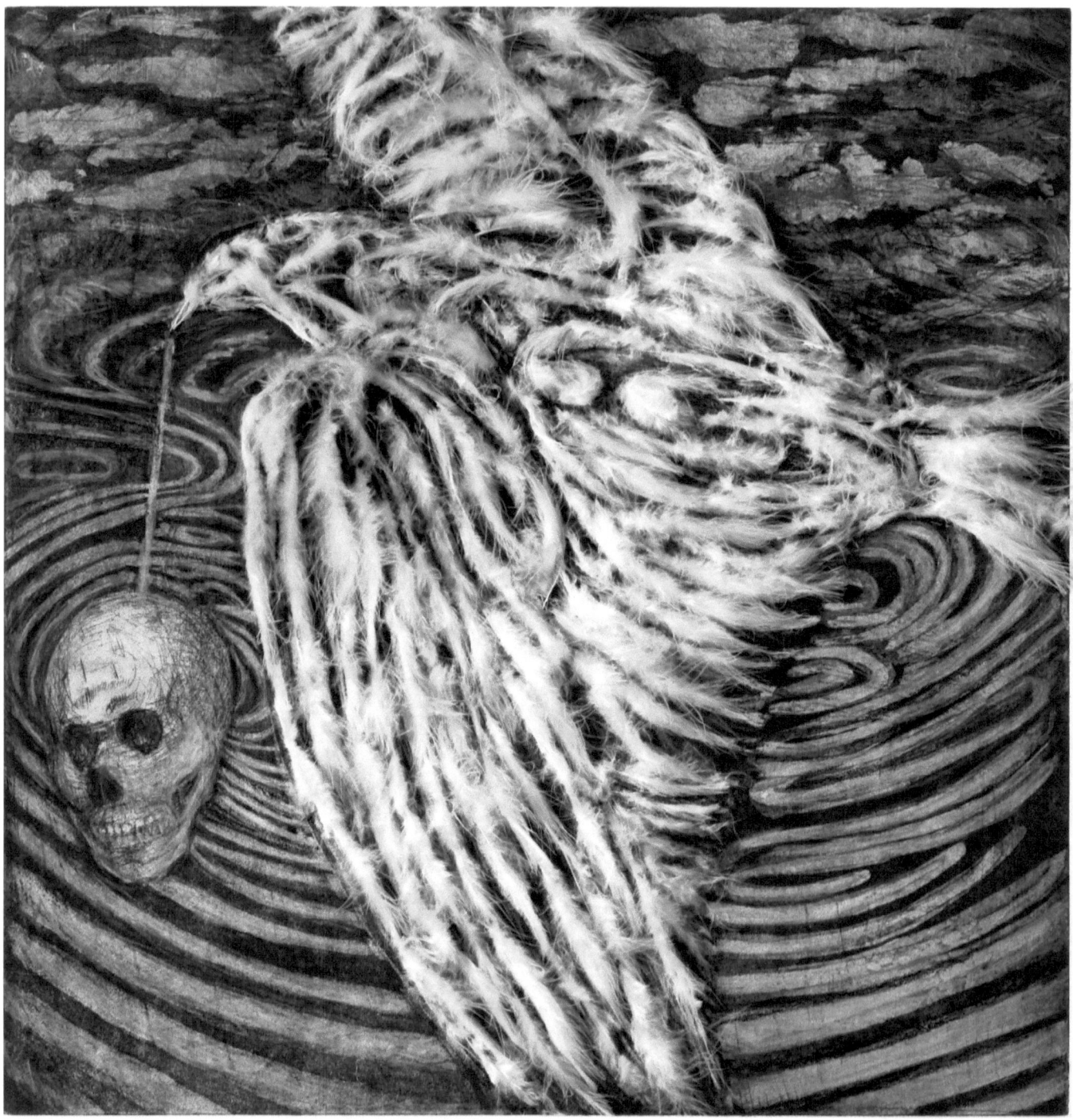

II

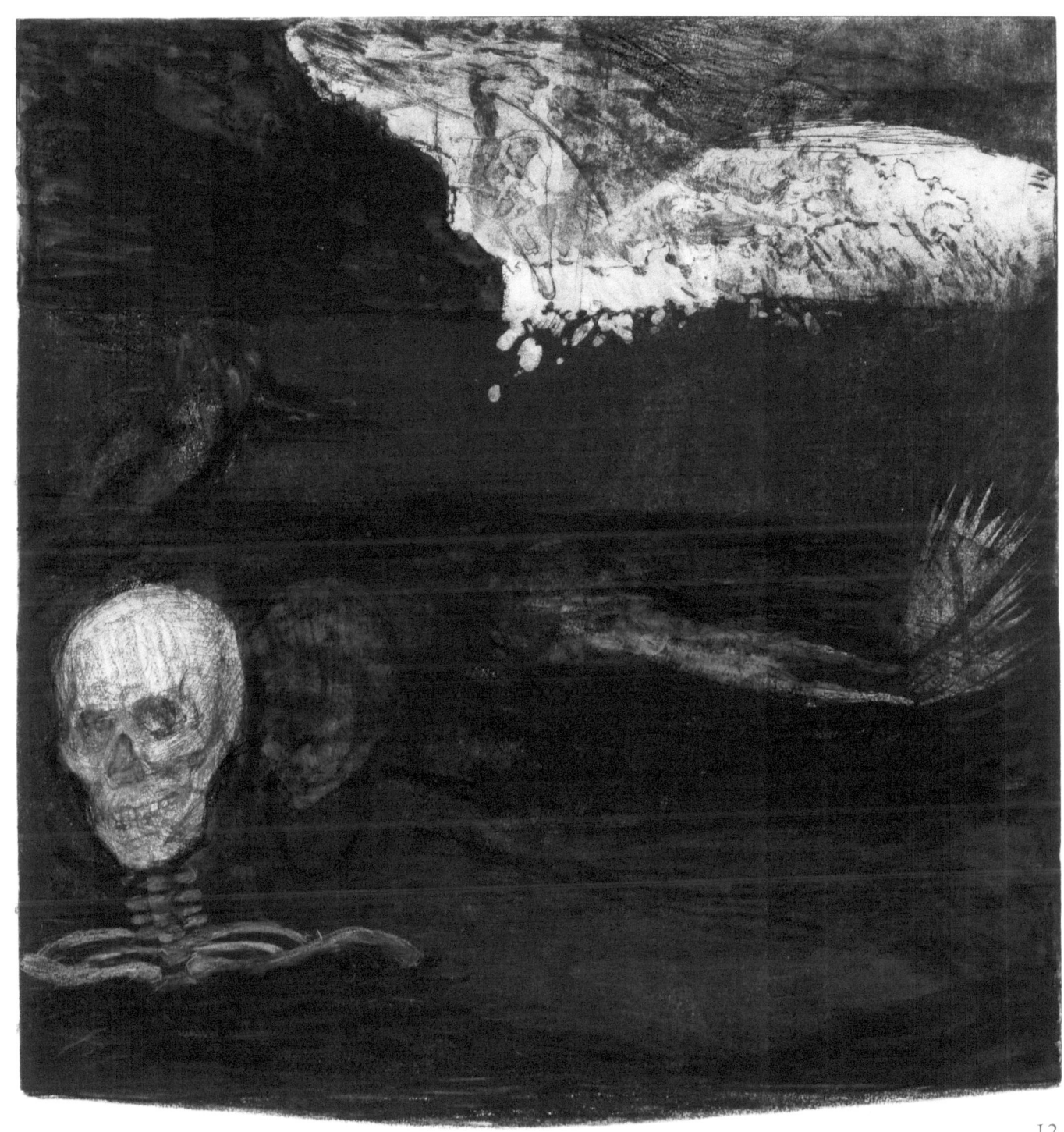

12

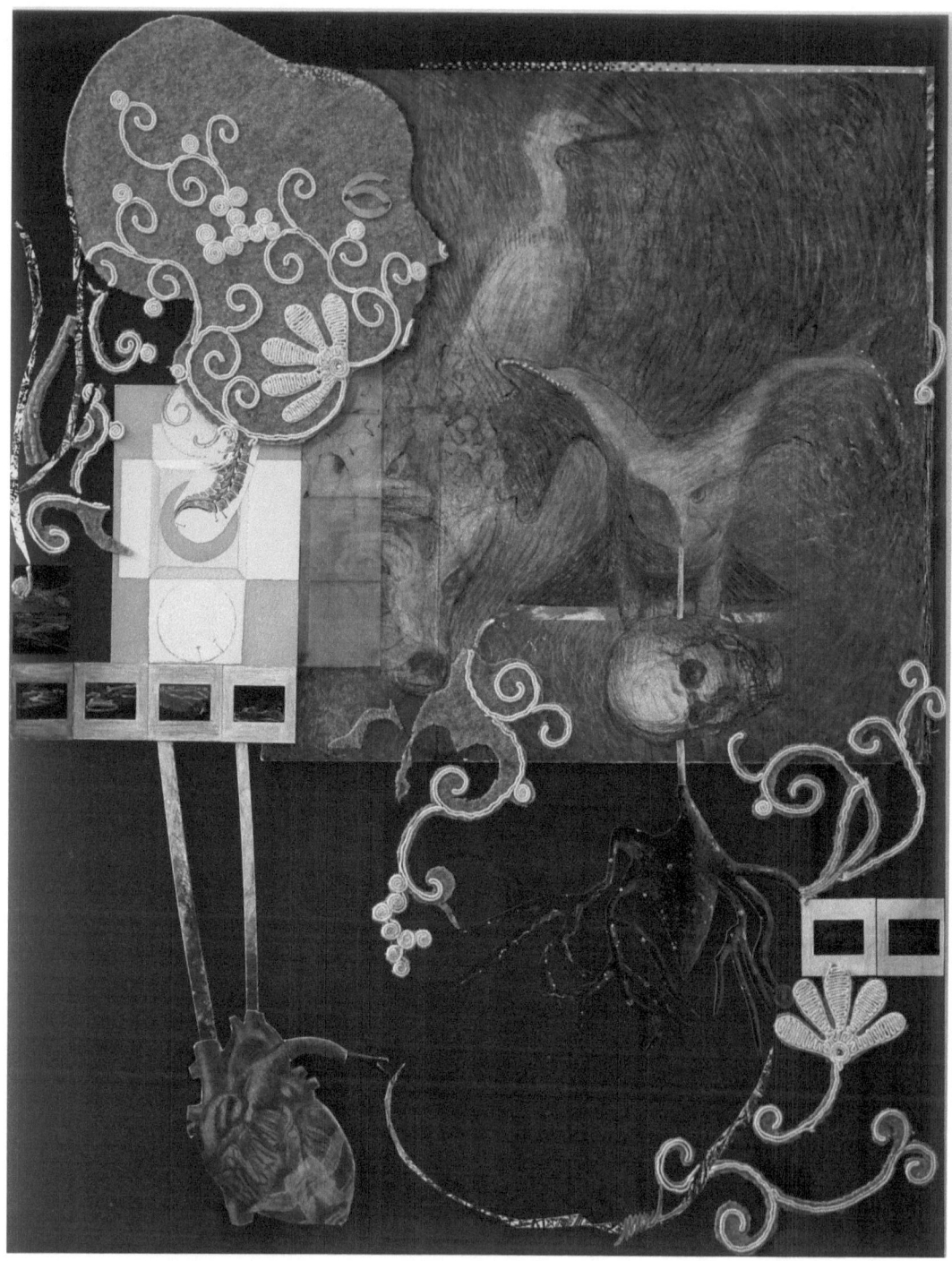

13

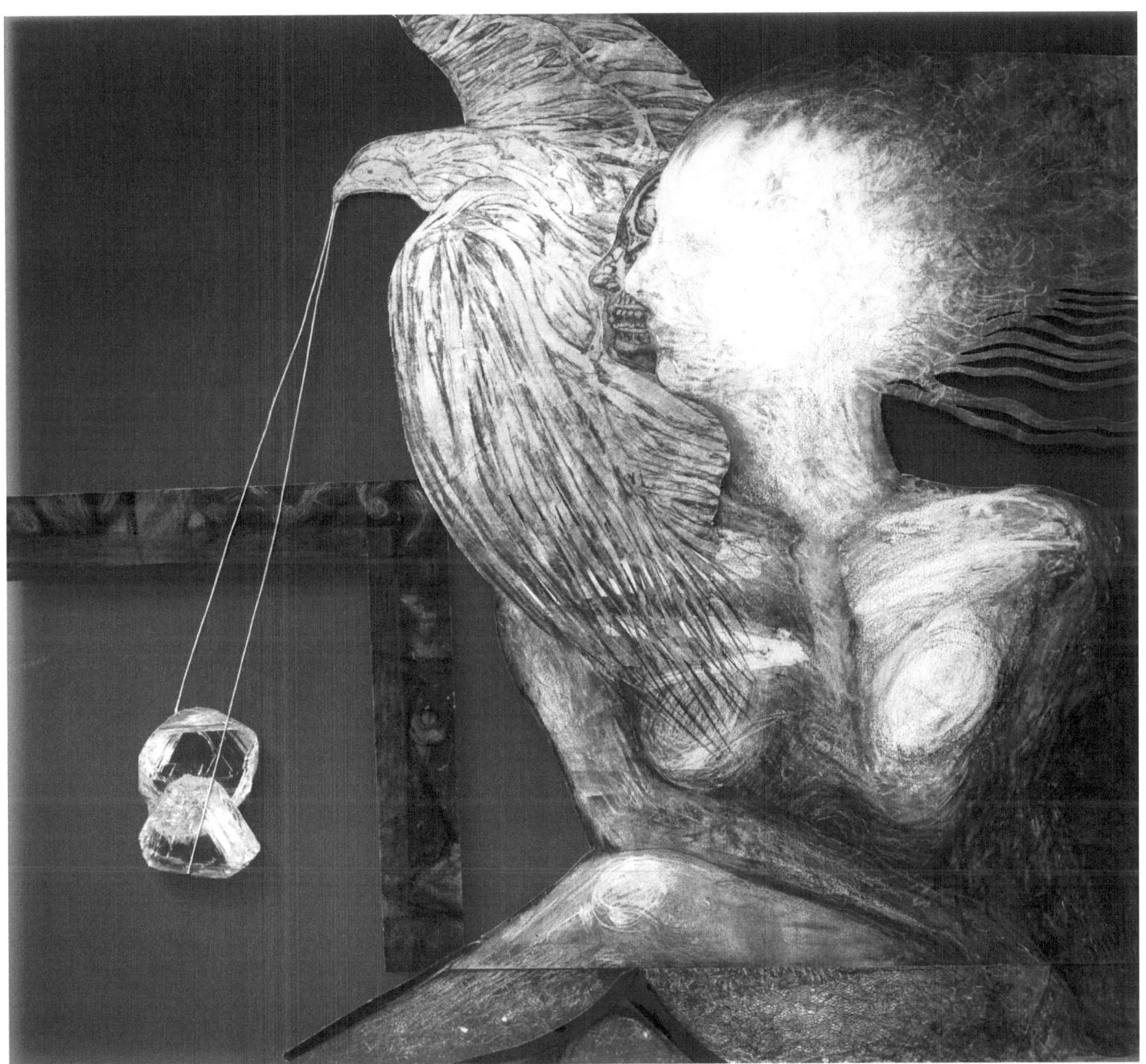

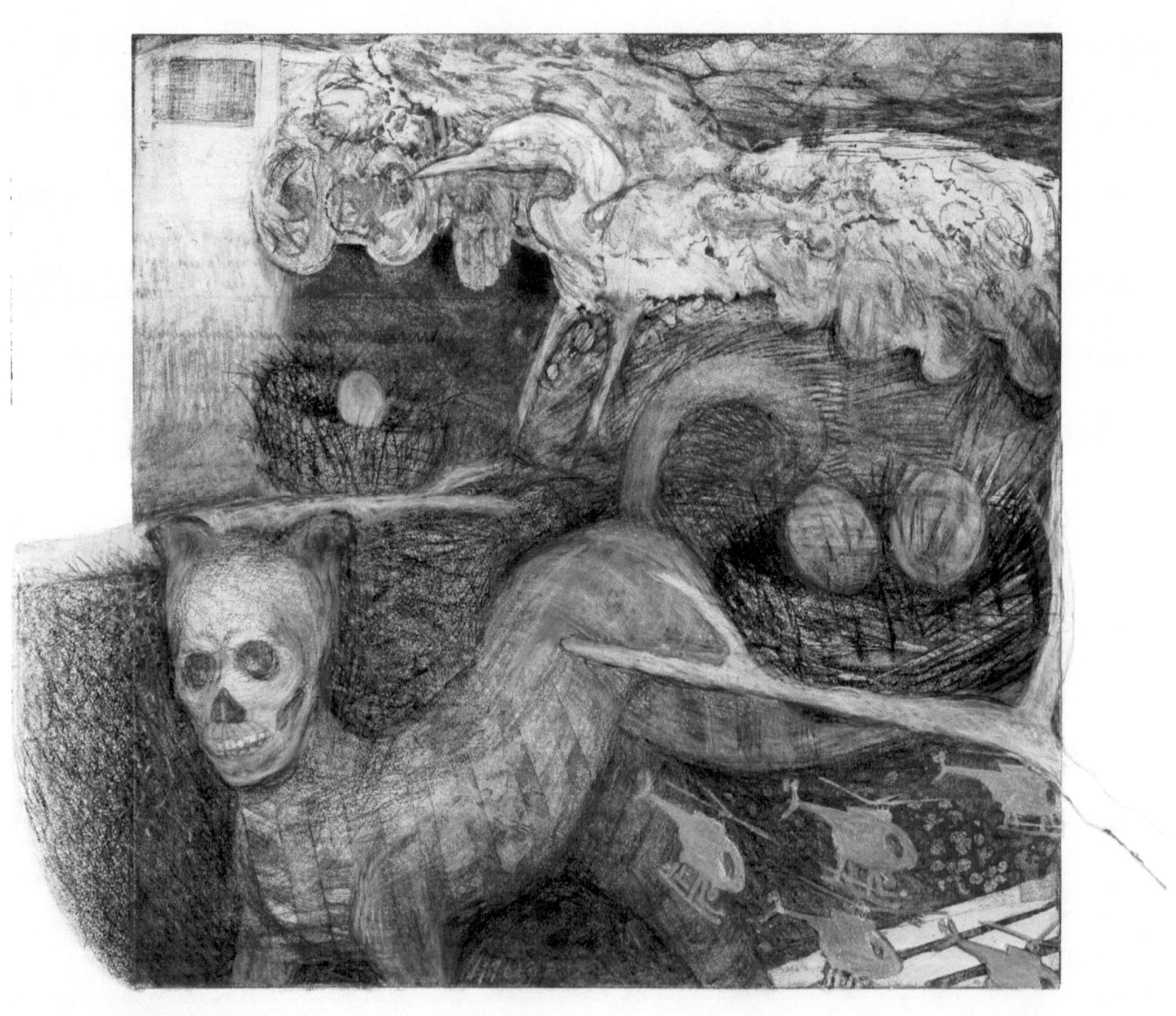

15

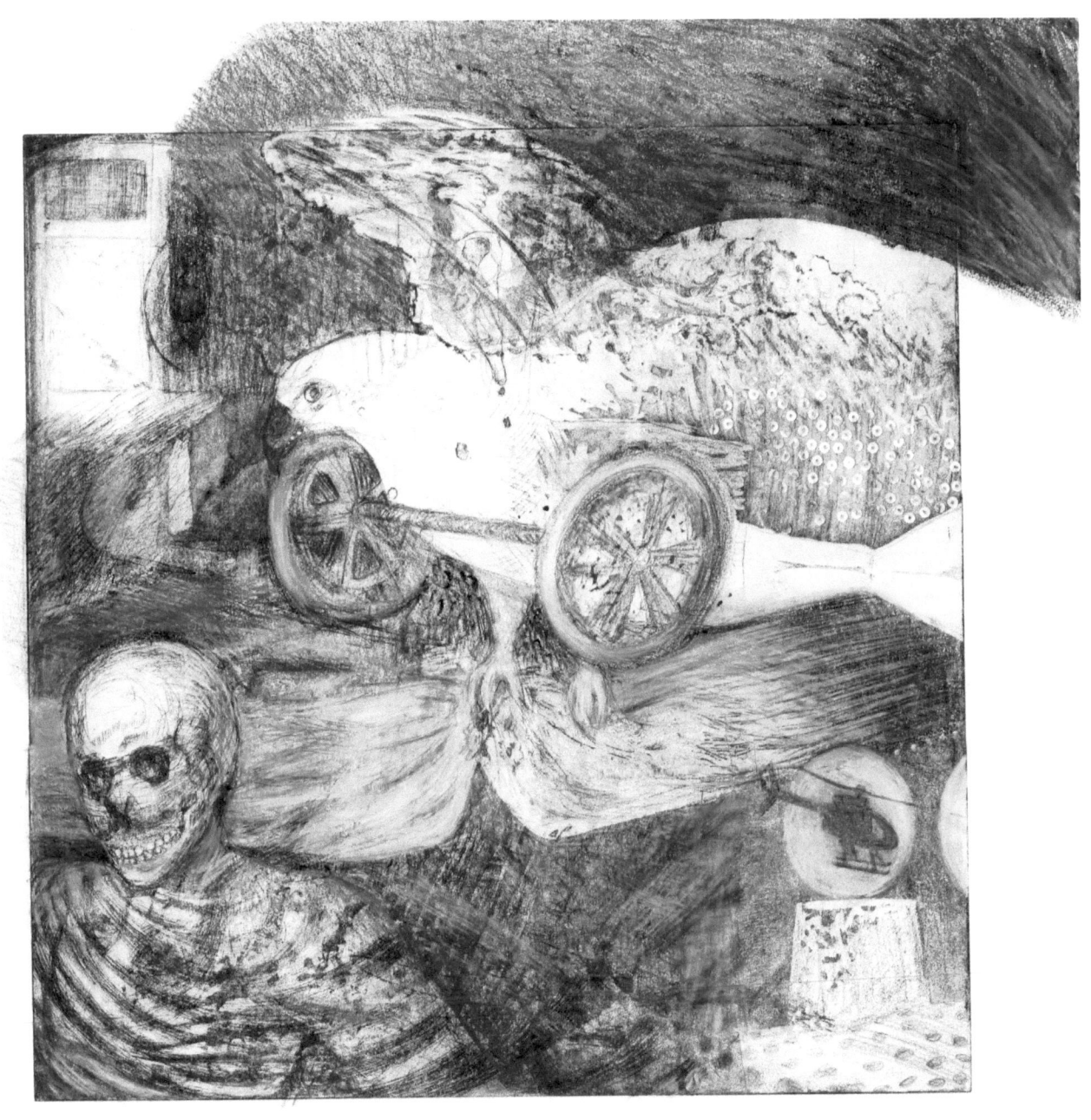

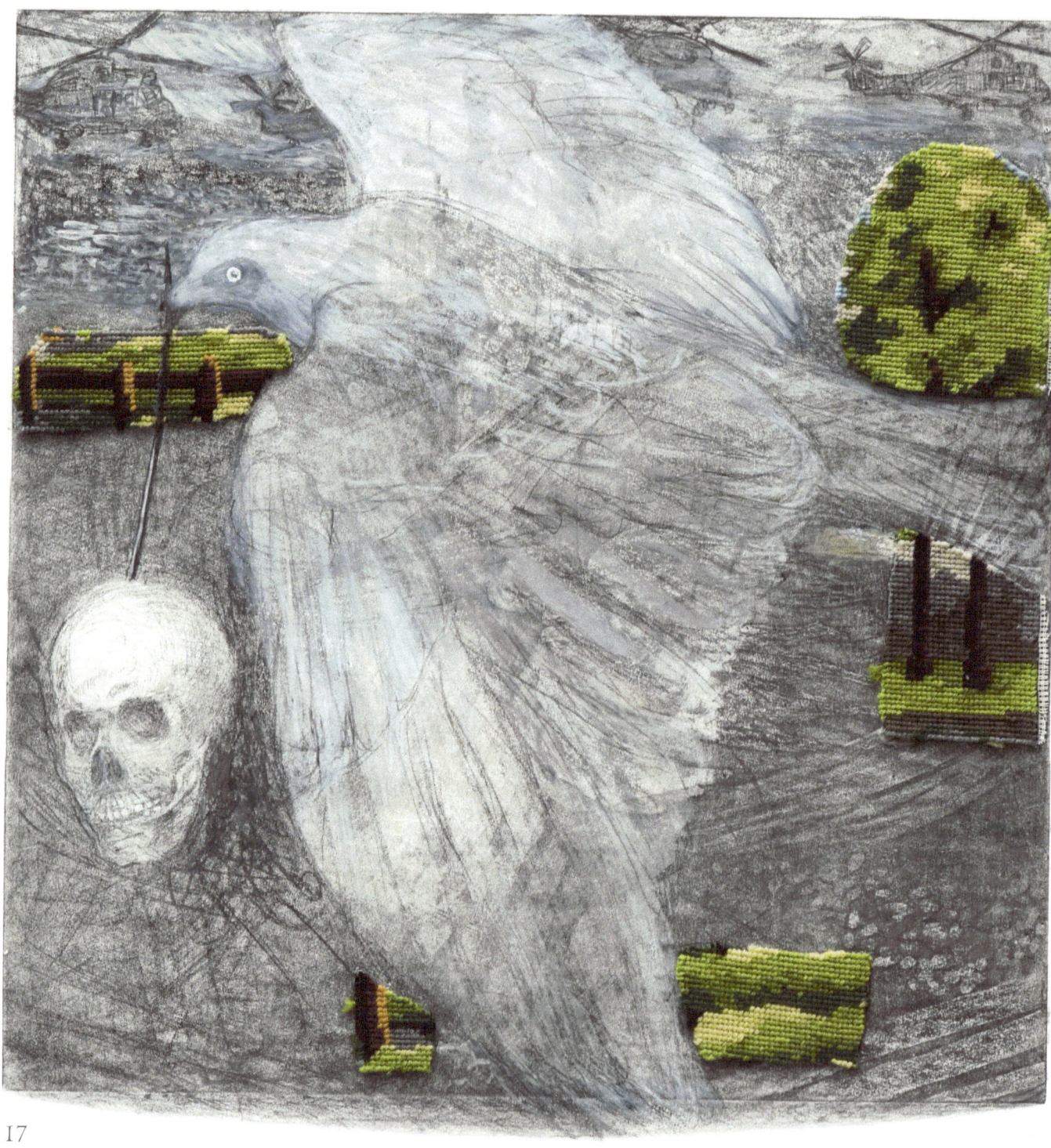

17

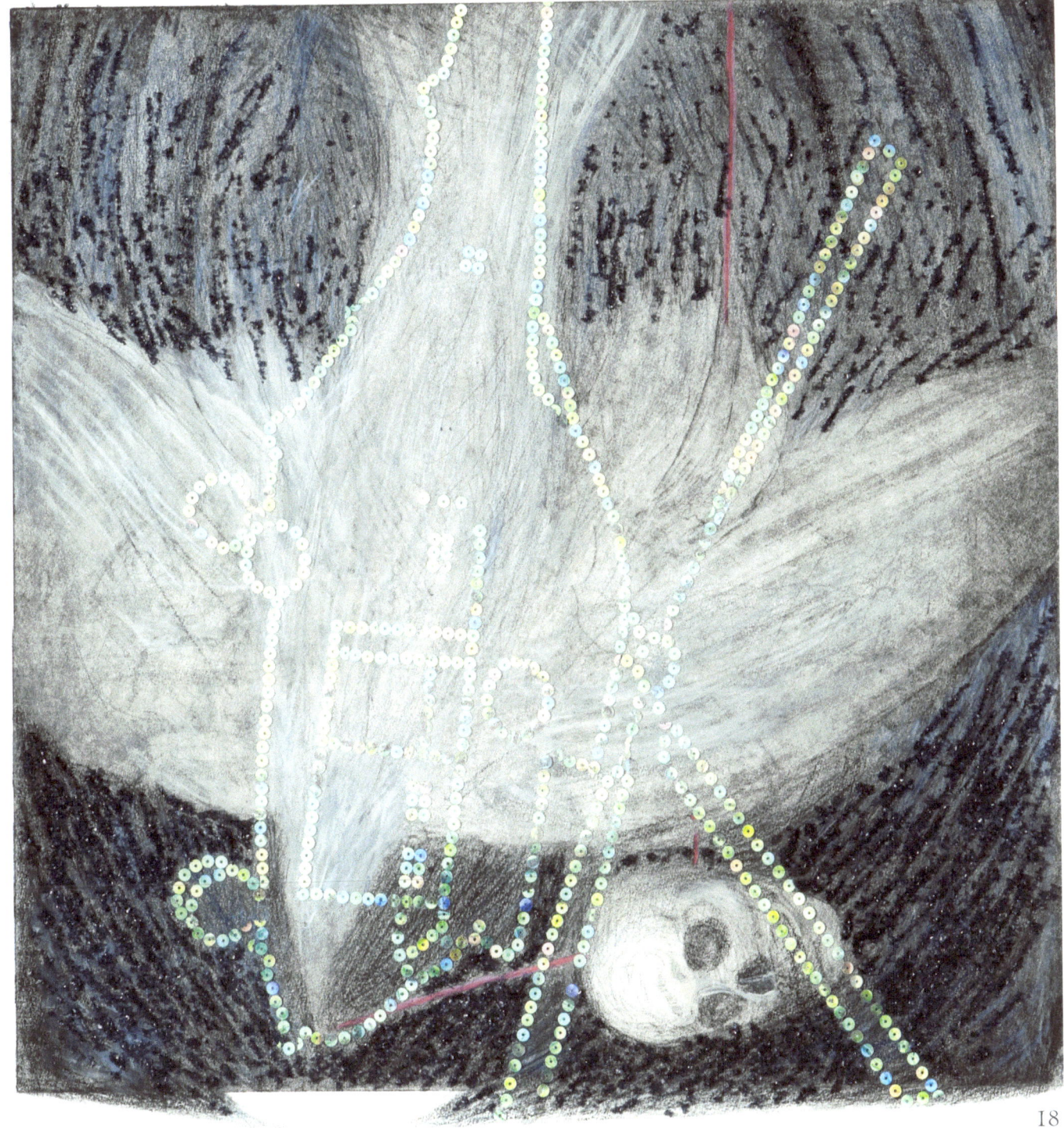

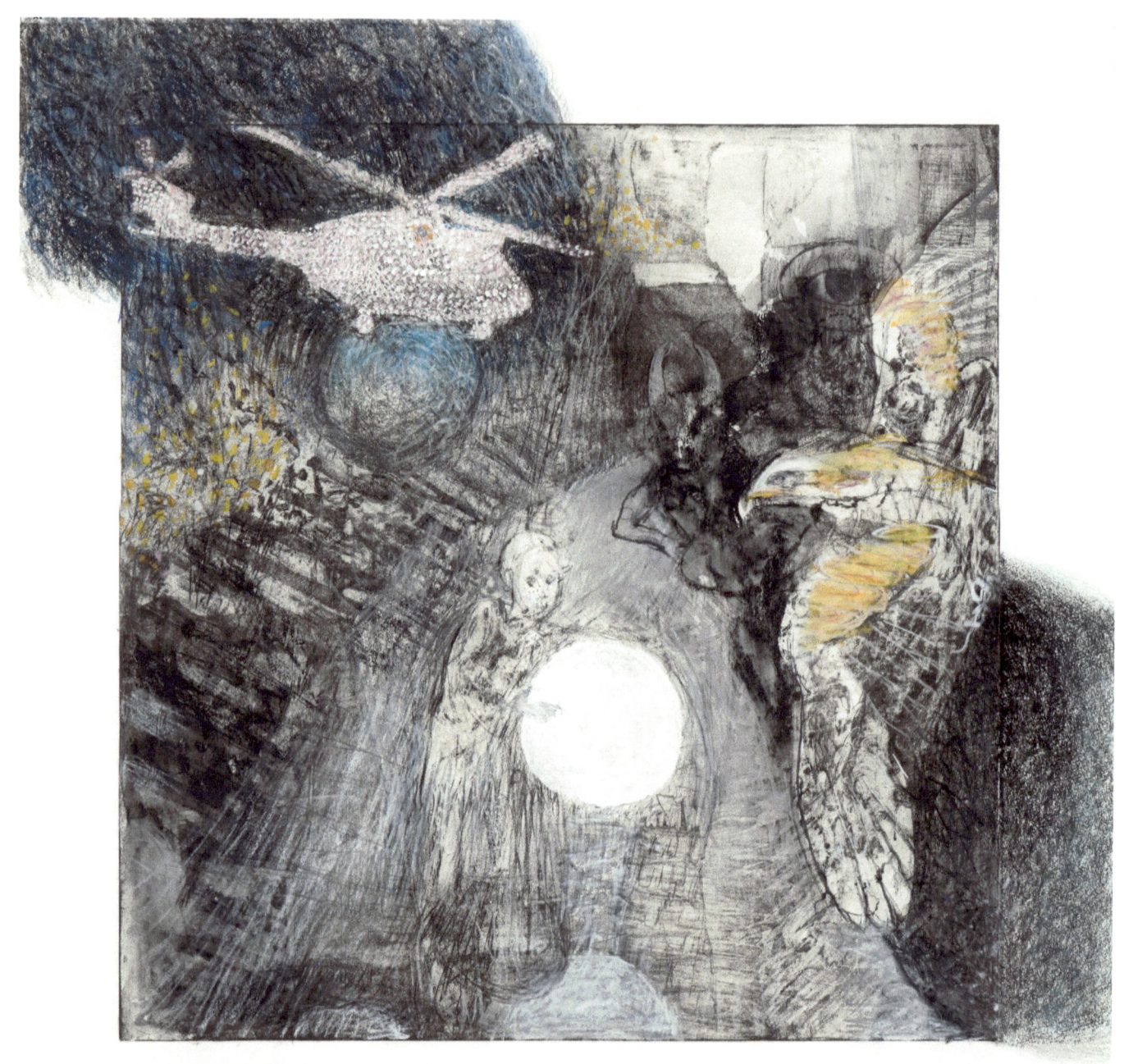

19

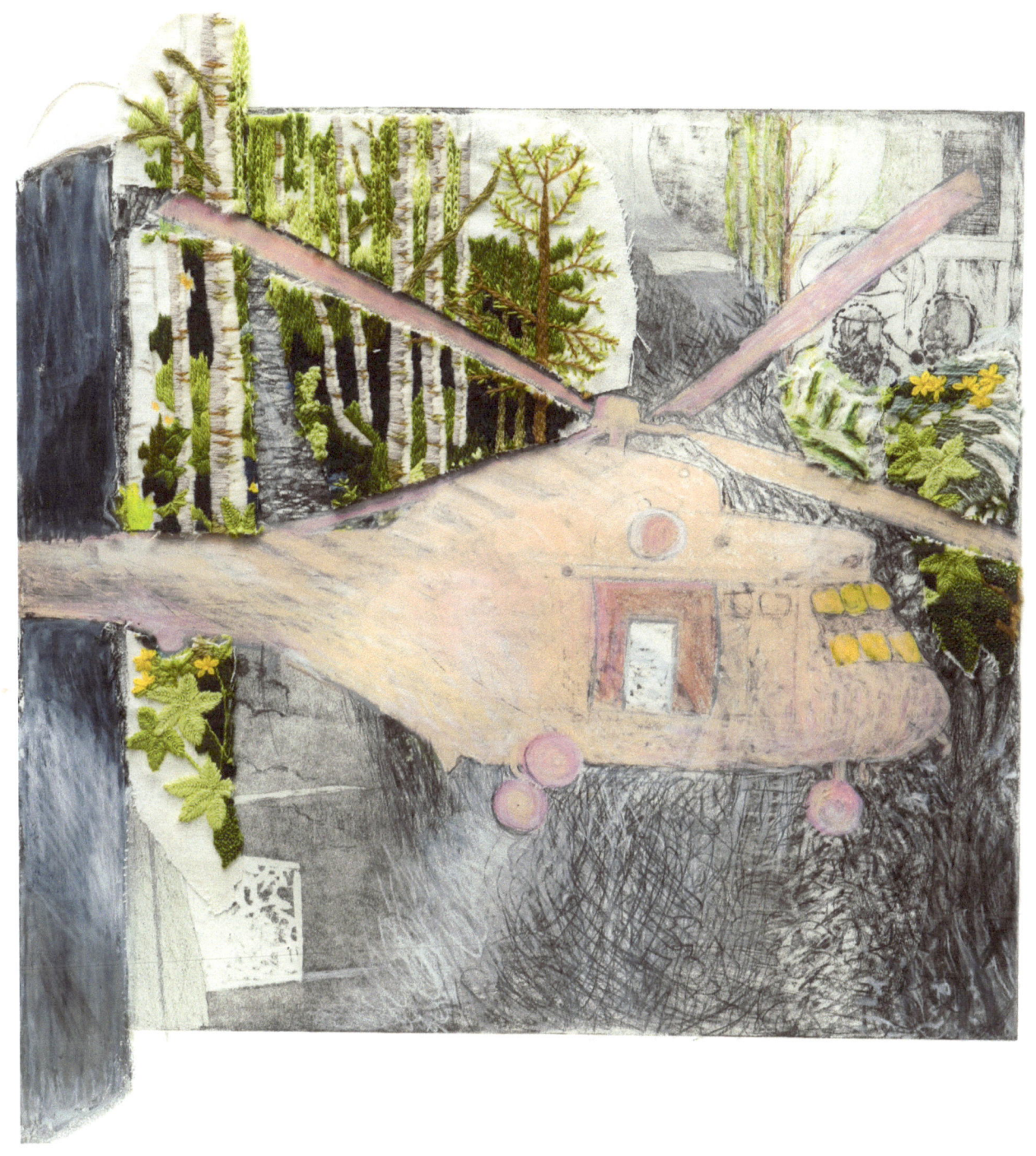

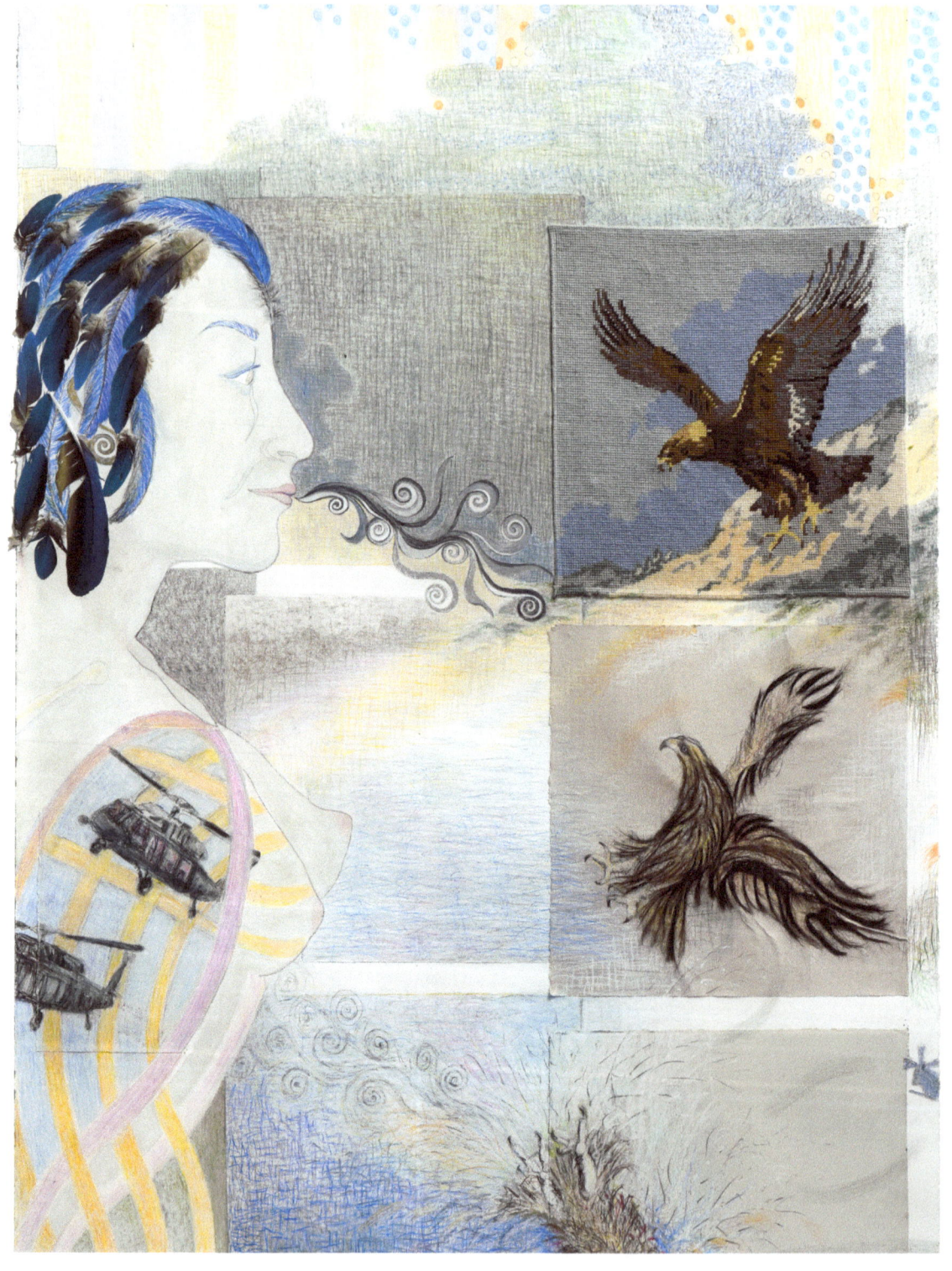

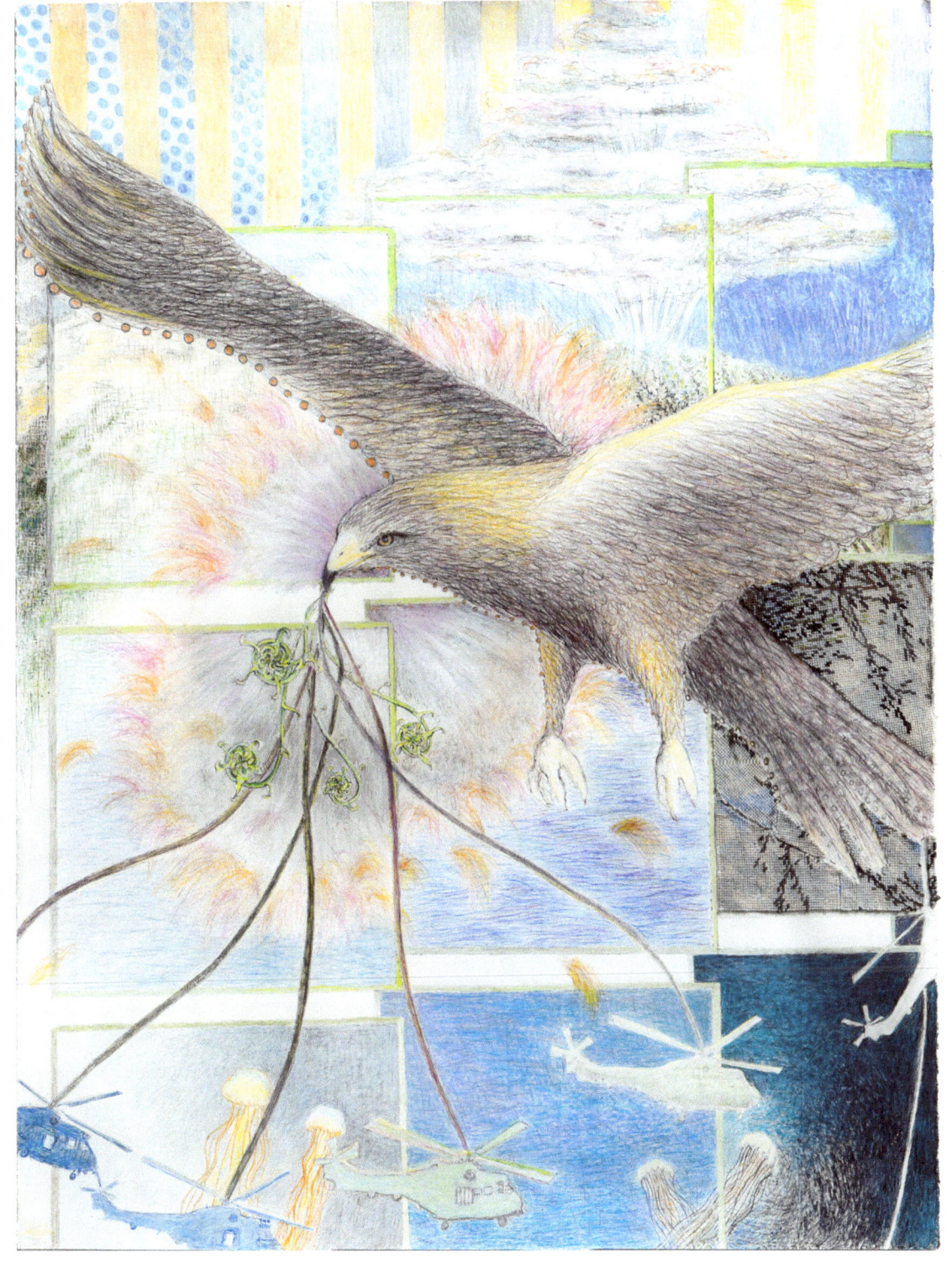

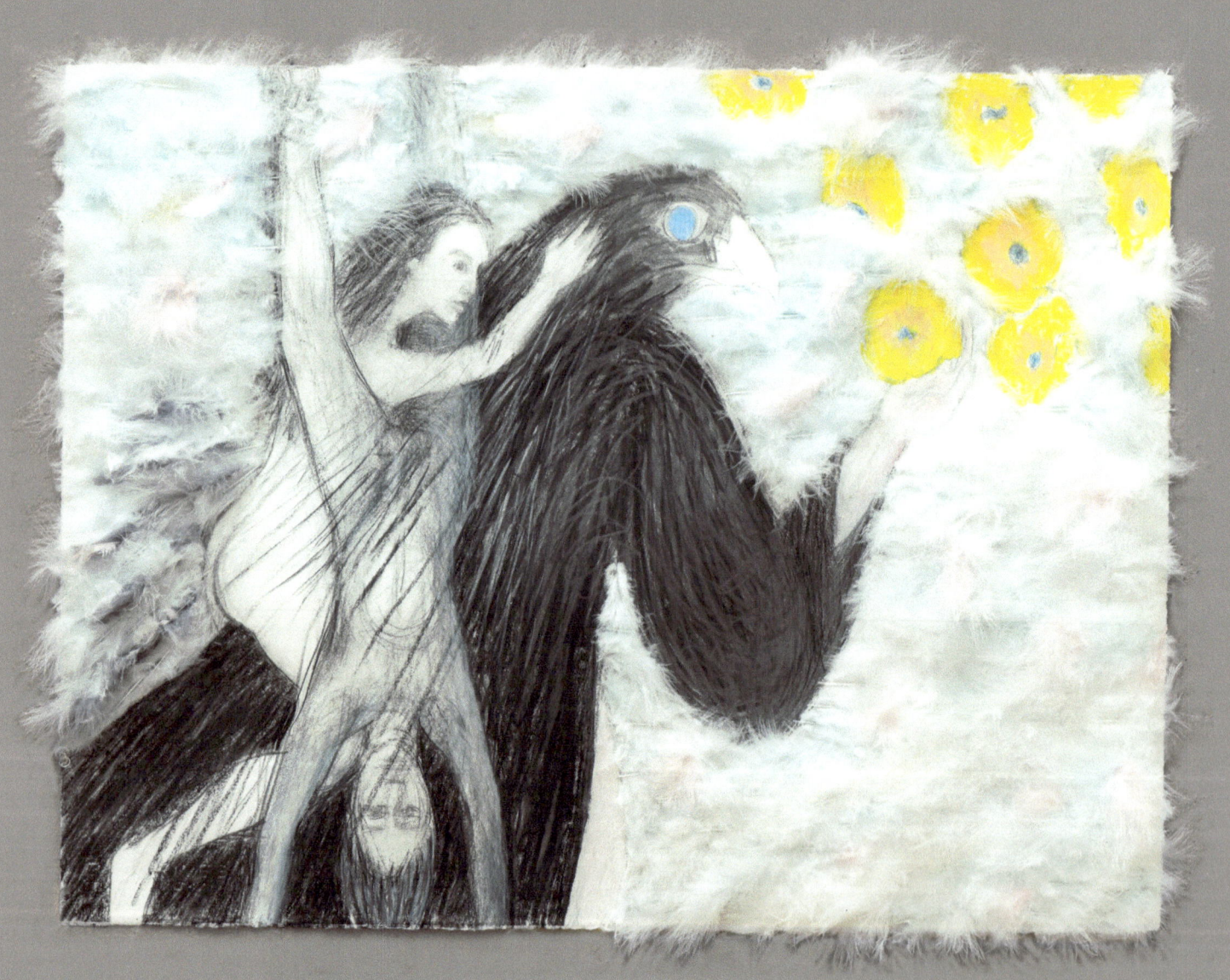

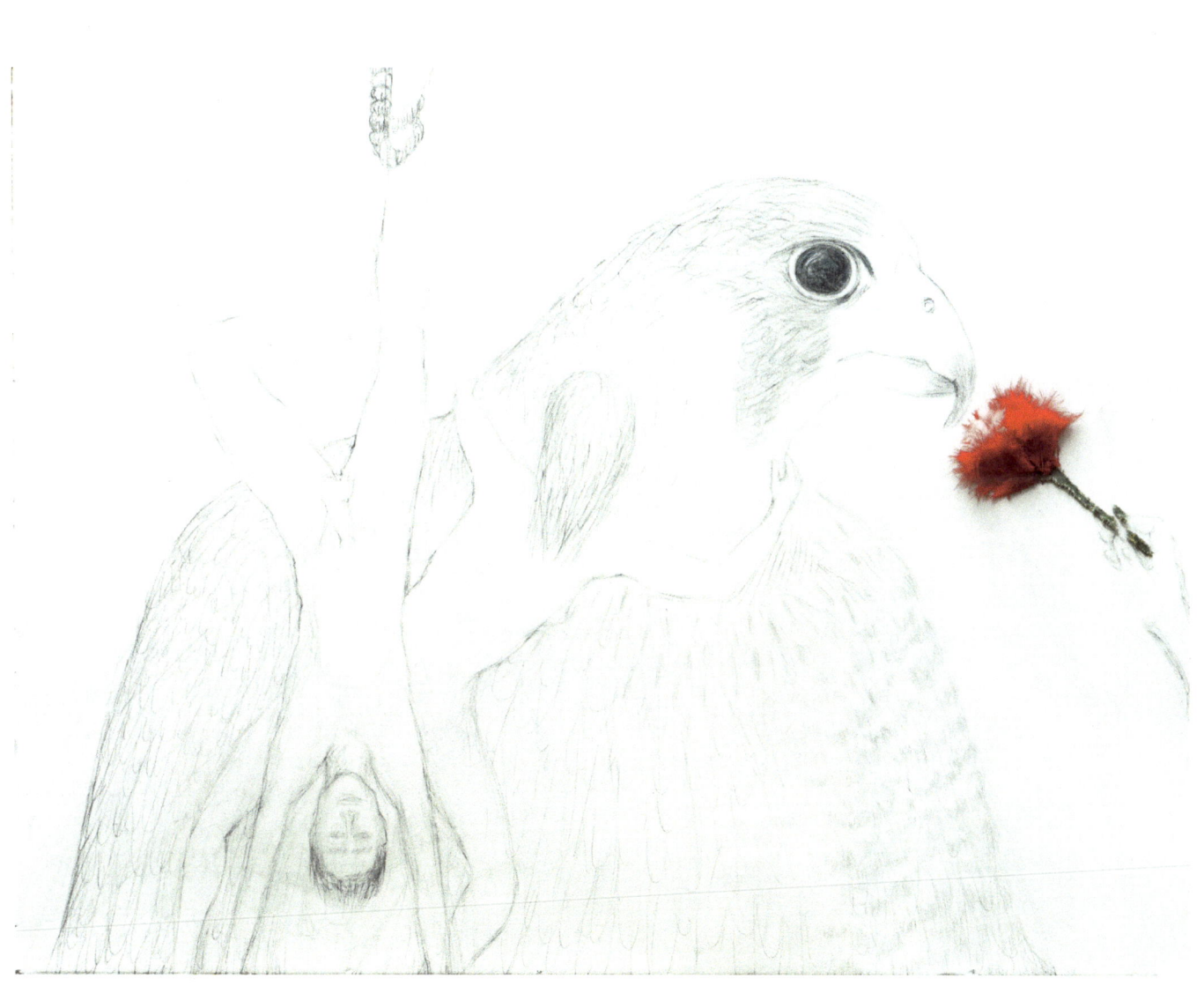

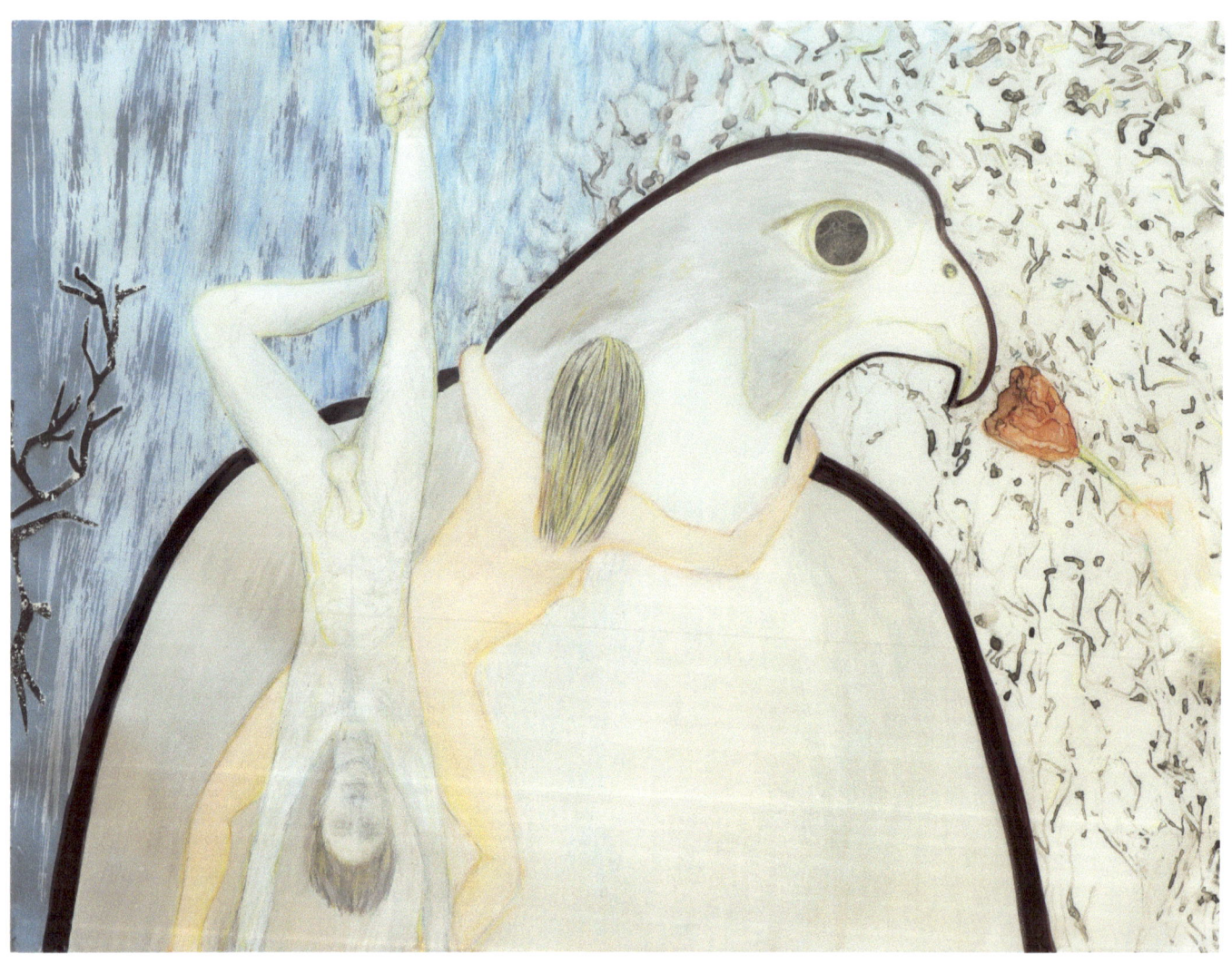

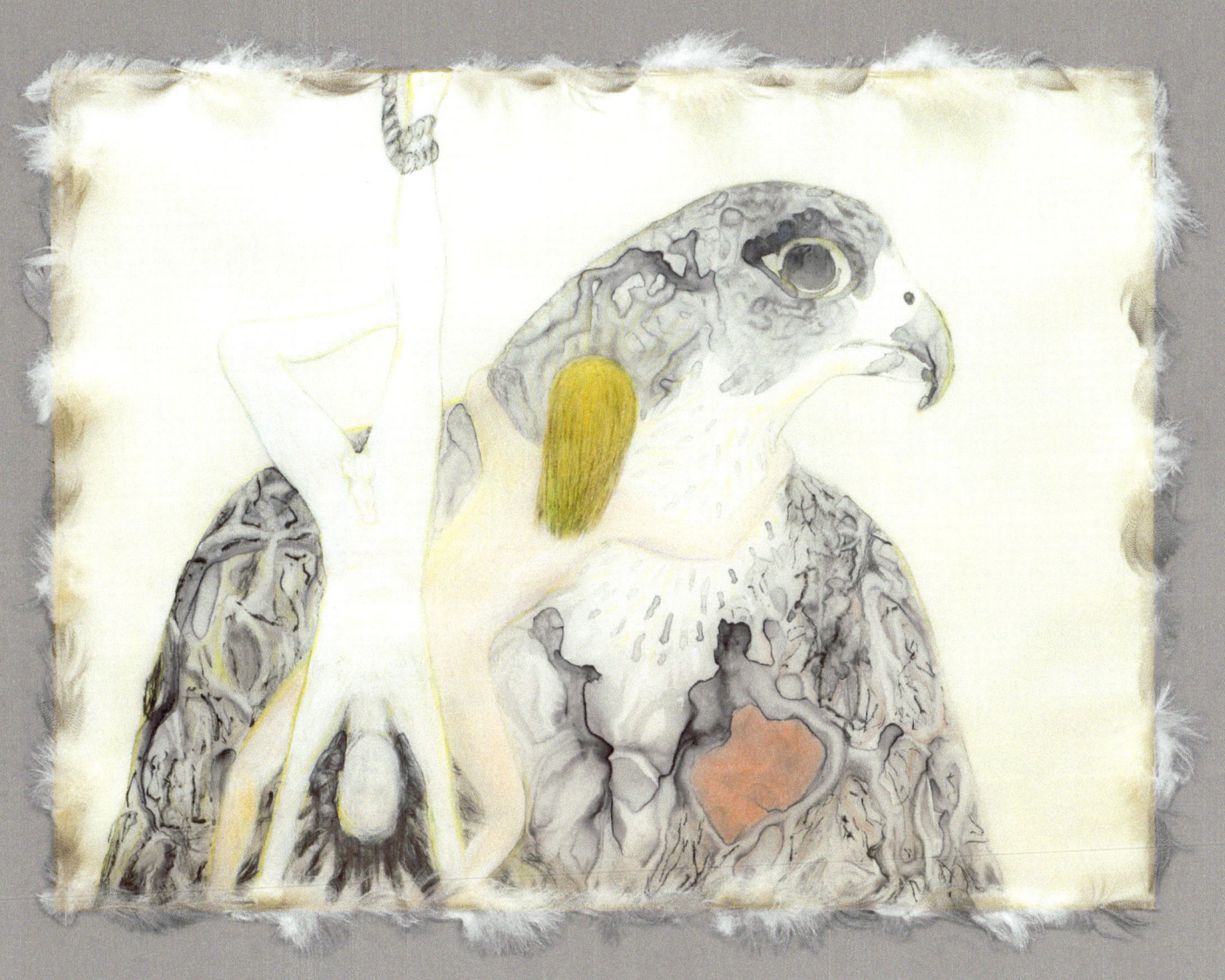

26

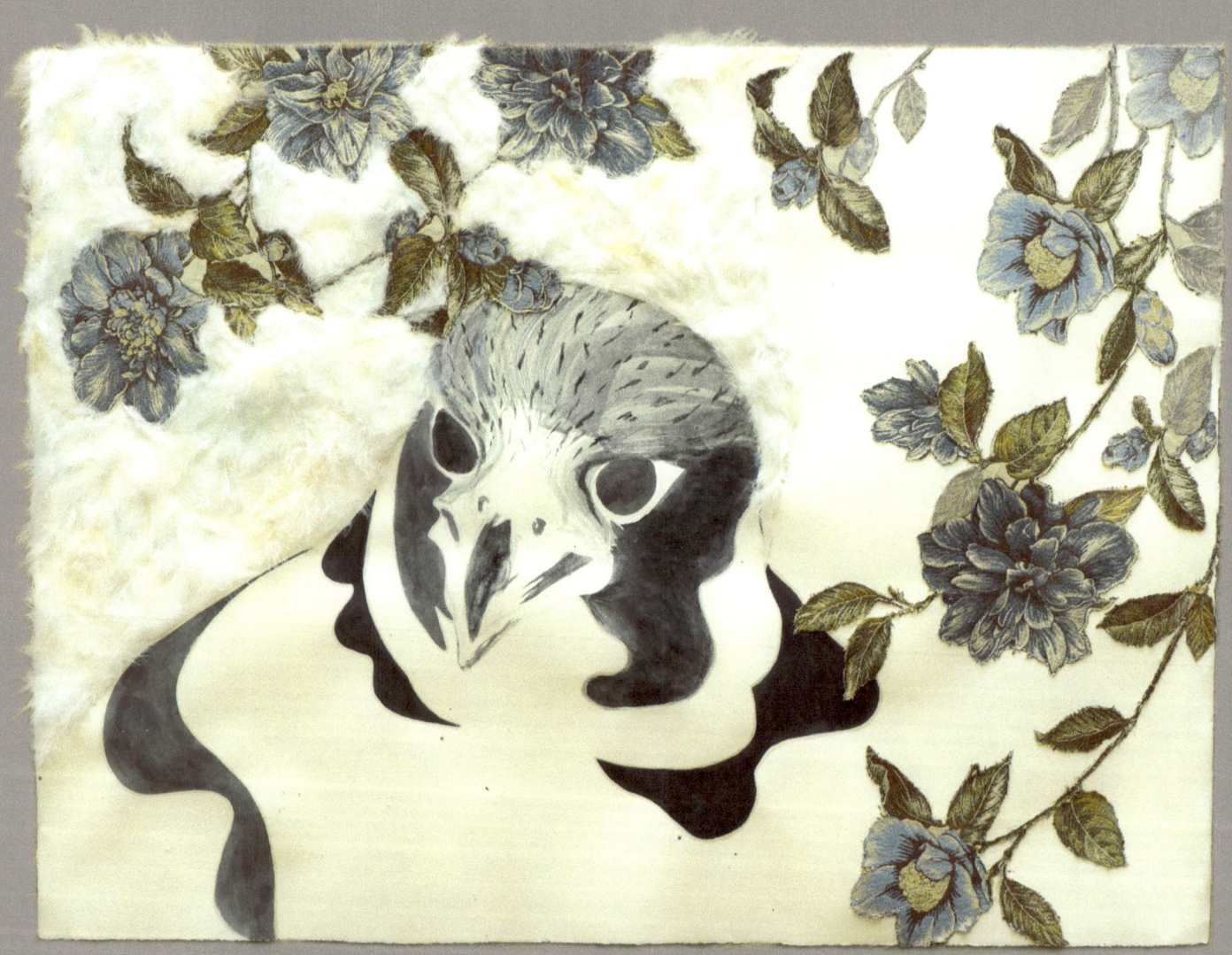

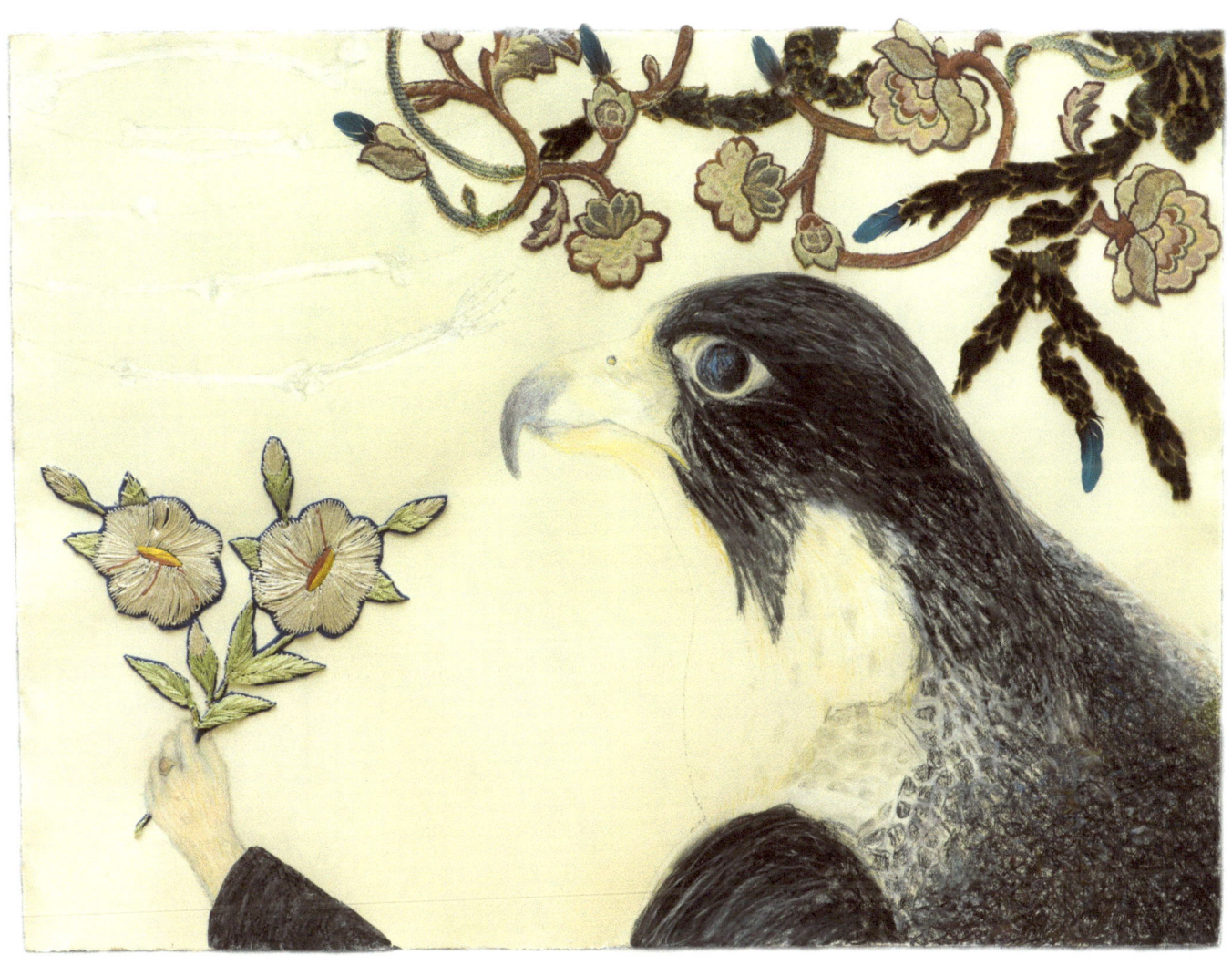

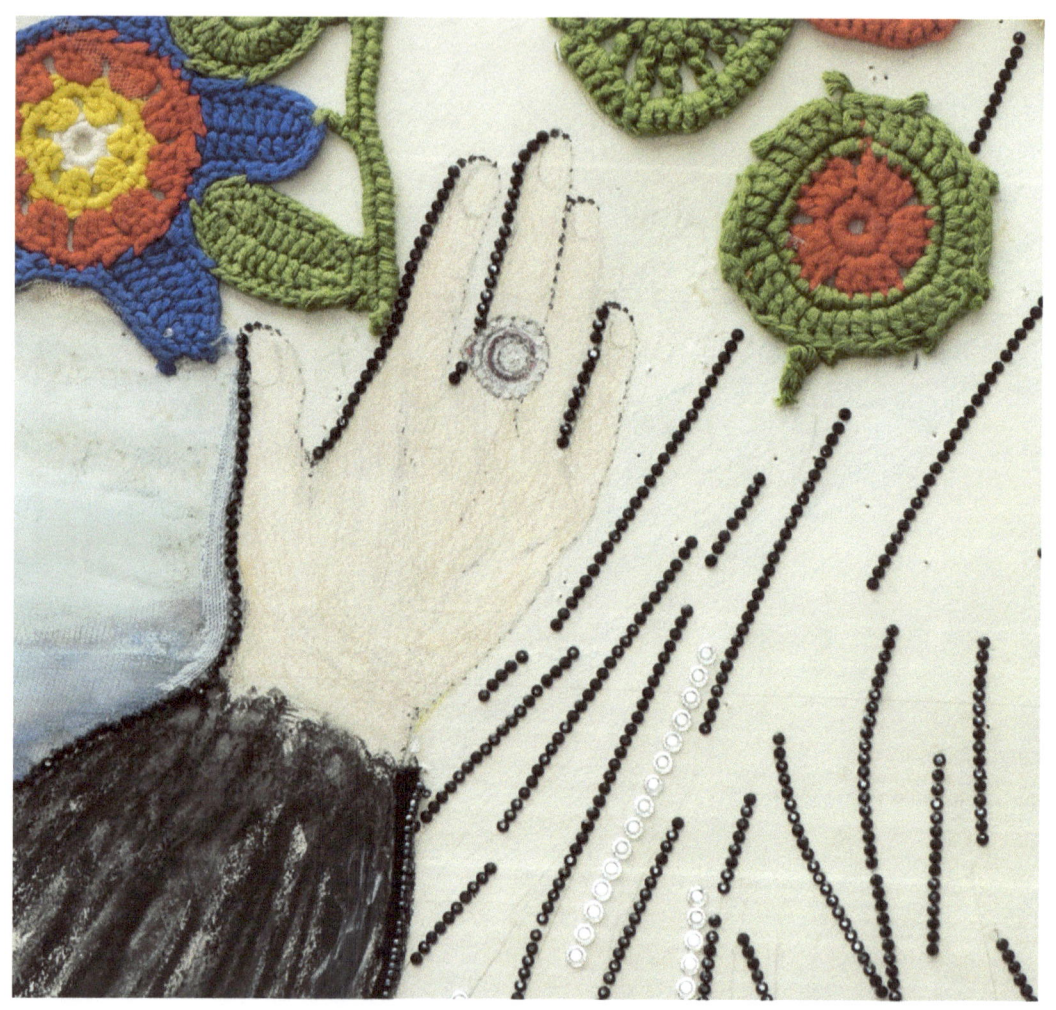

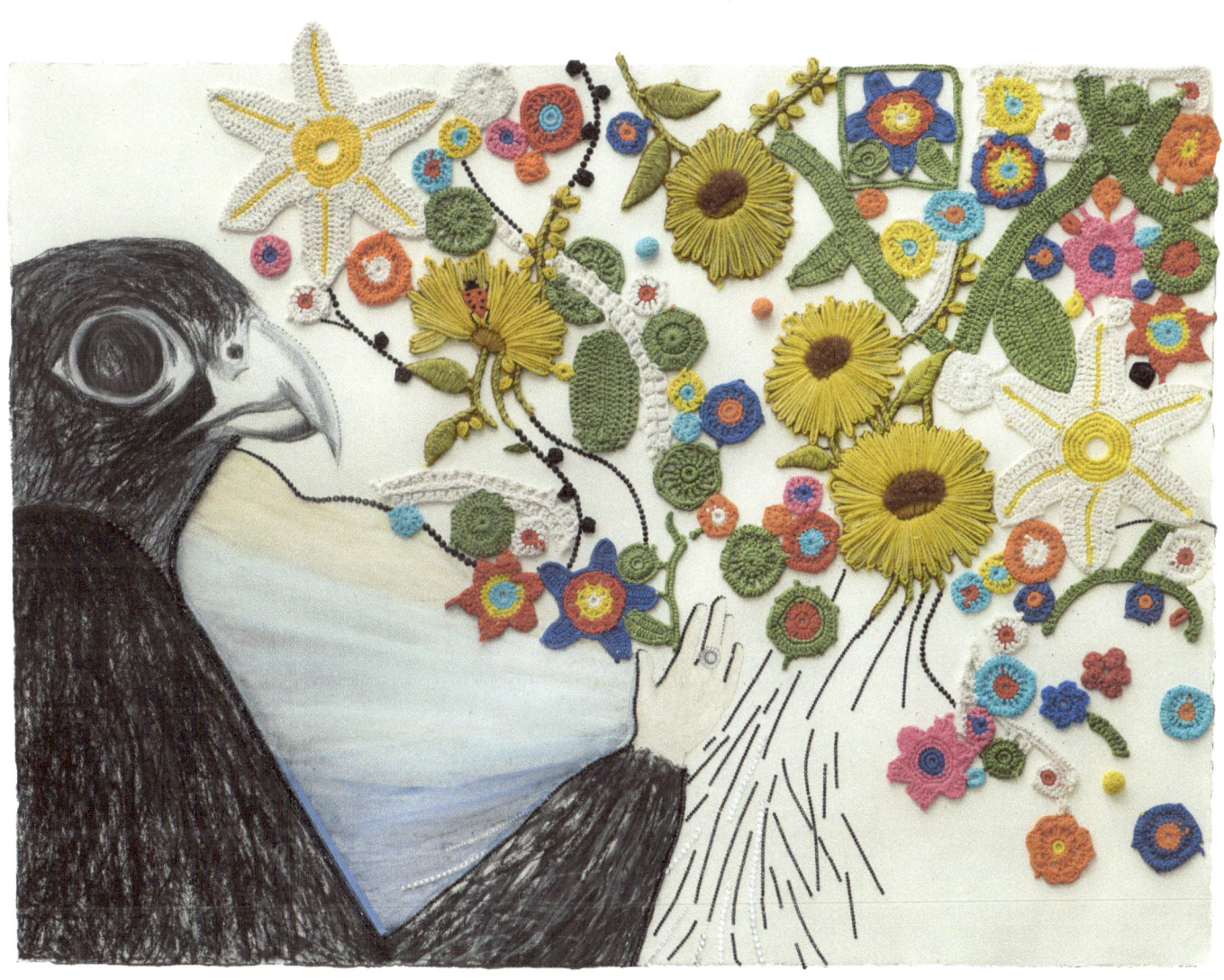

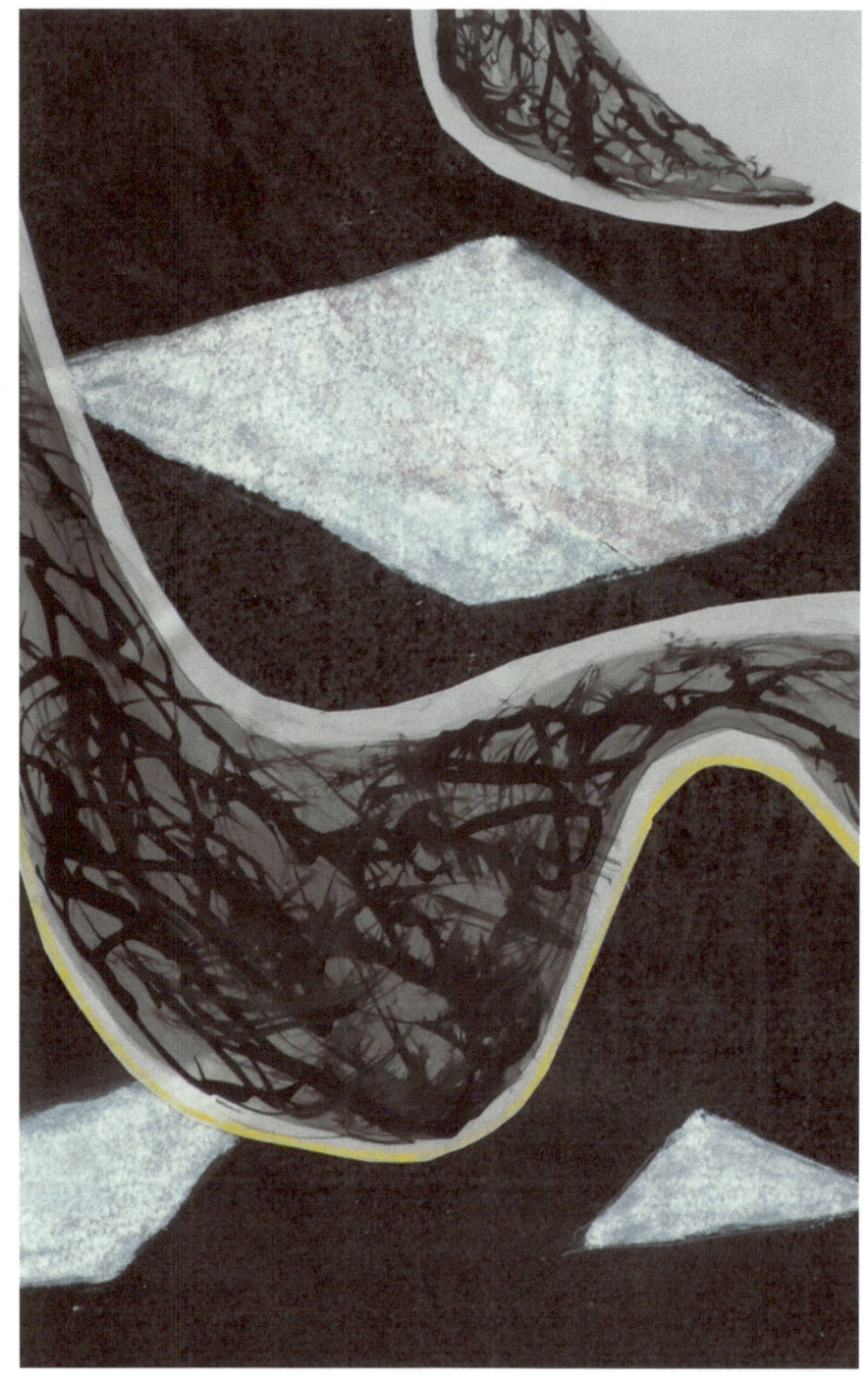

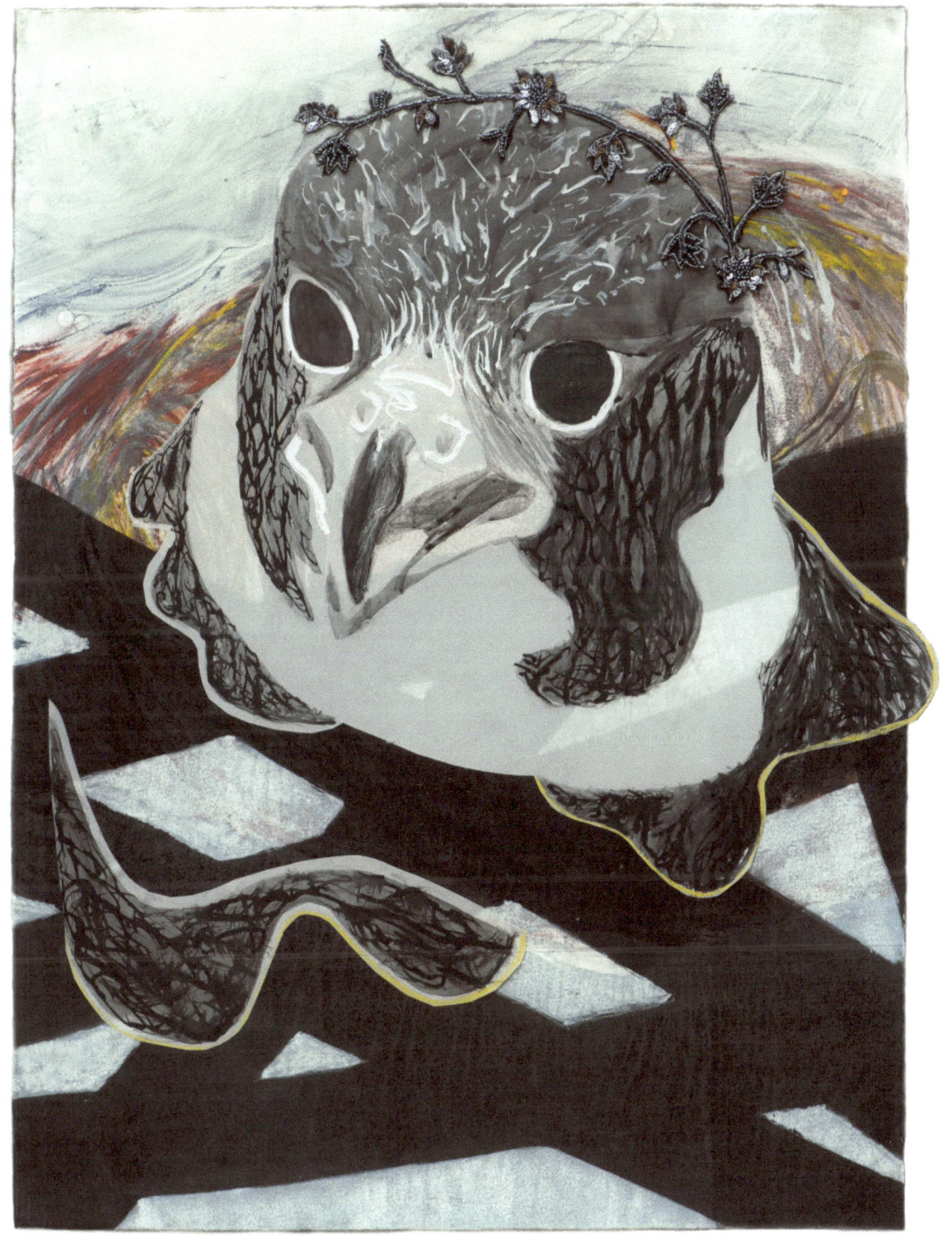

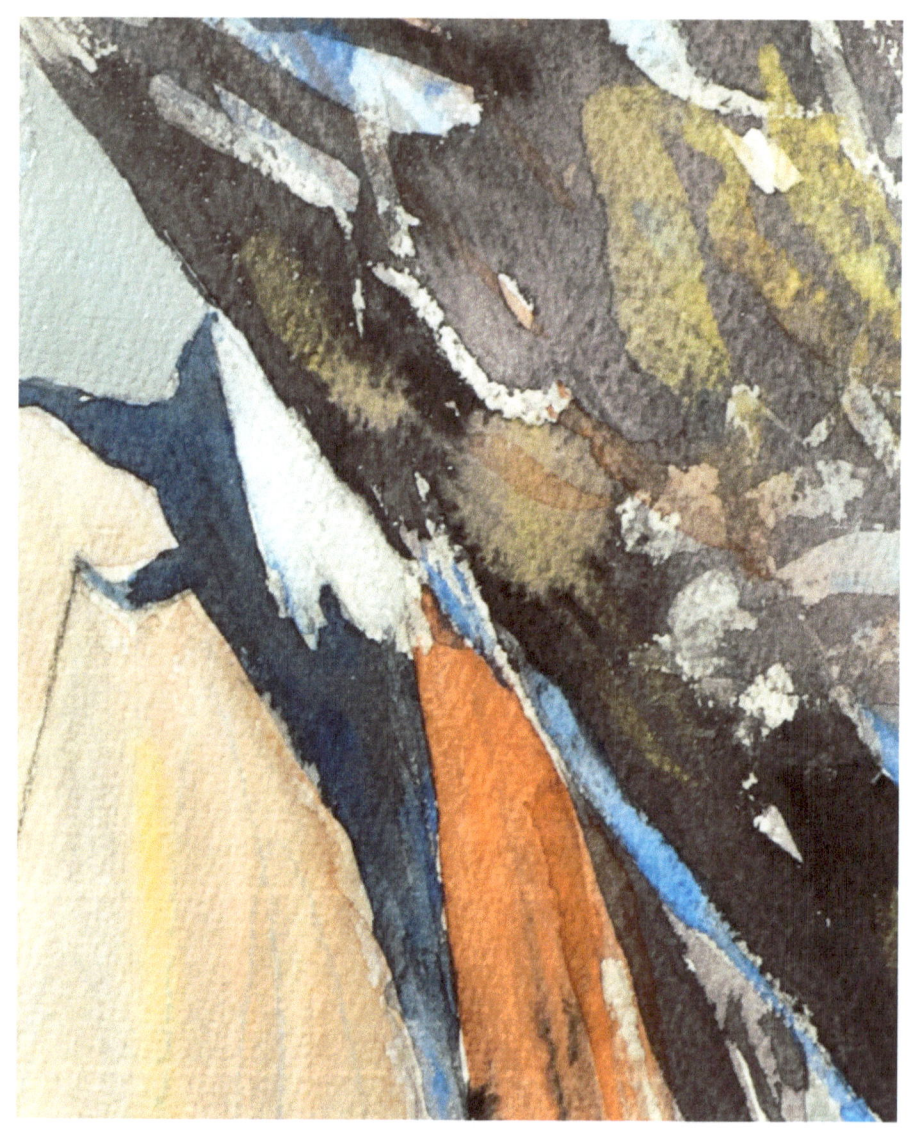

33

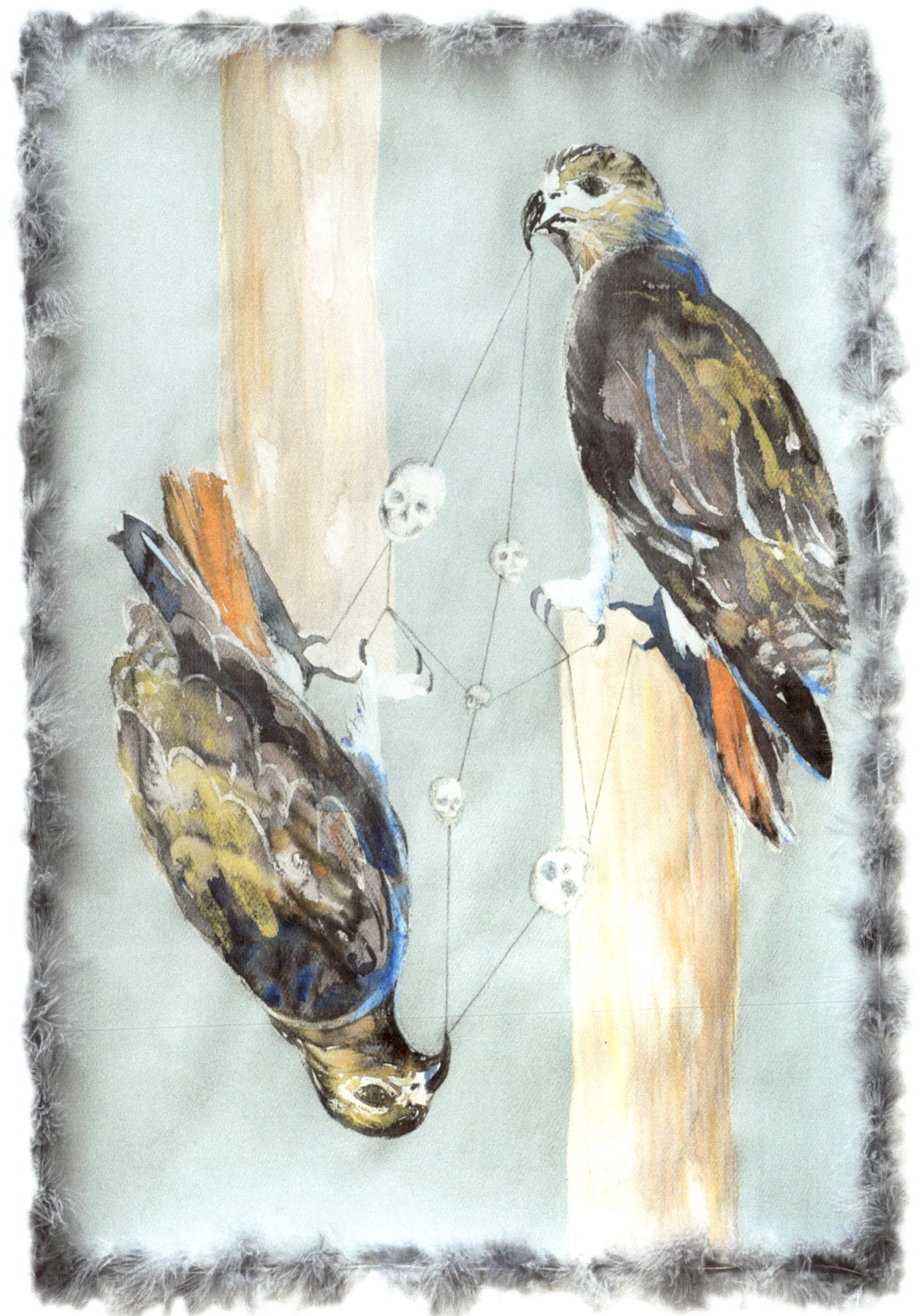

34

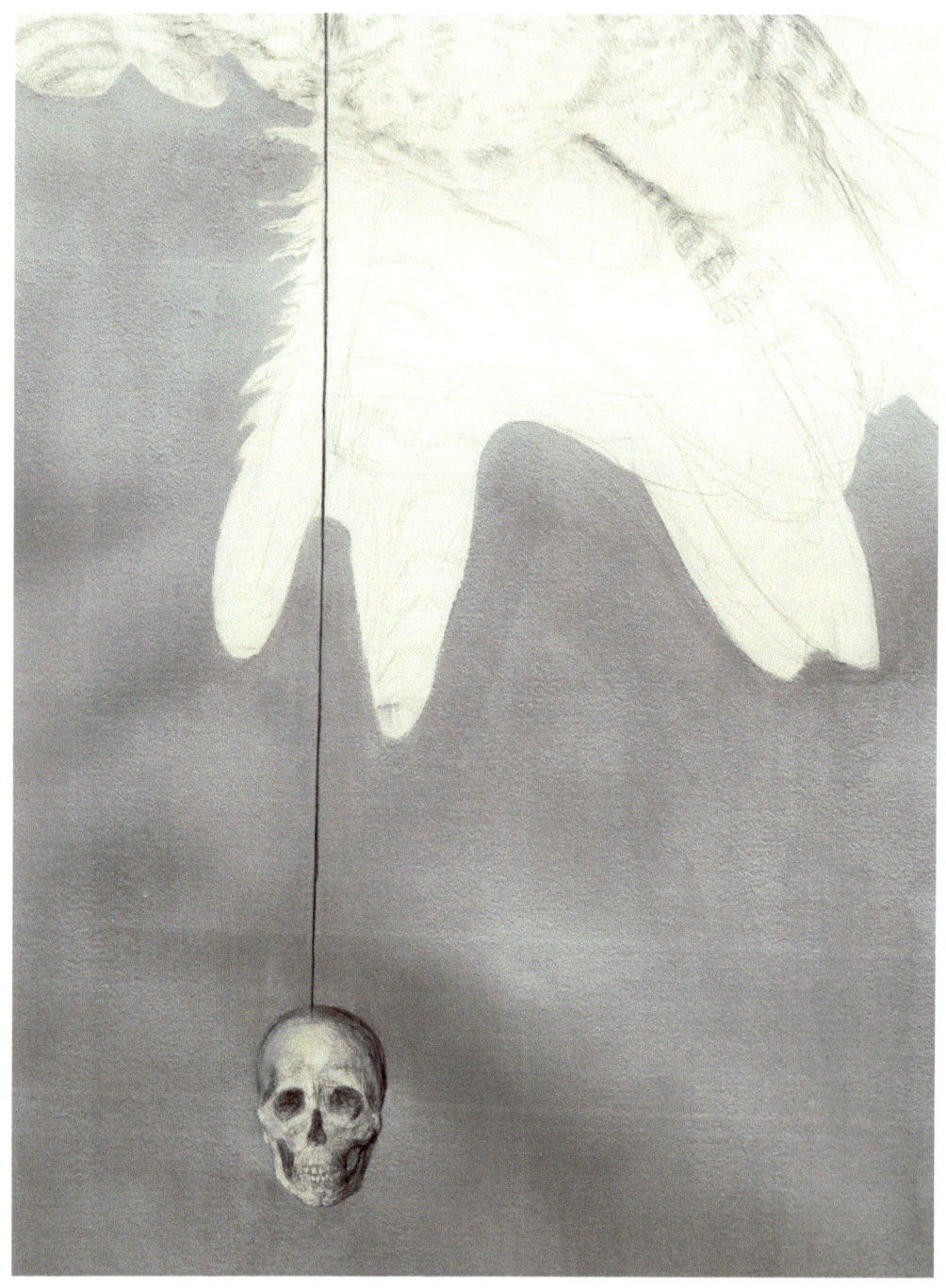

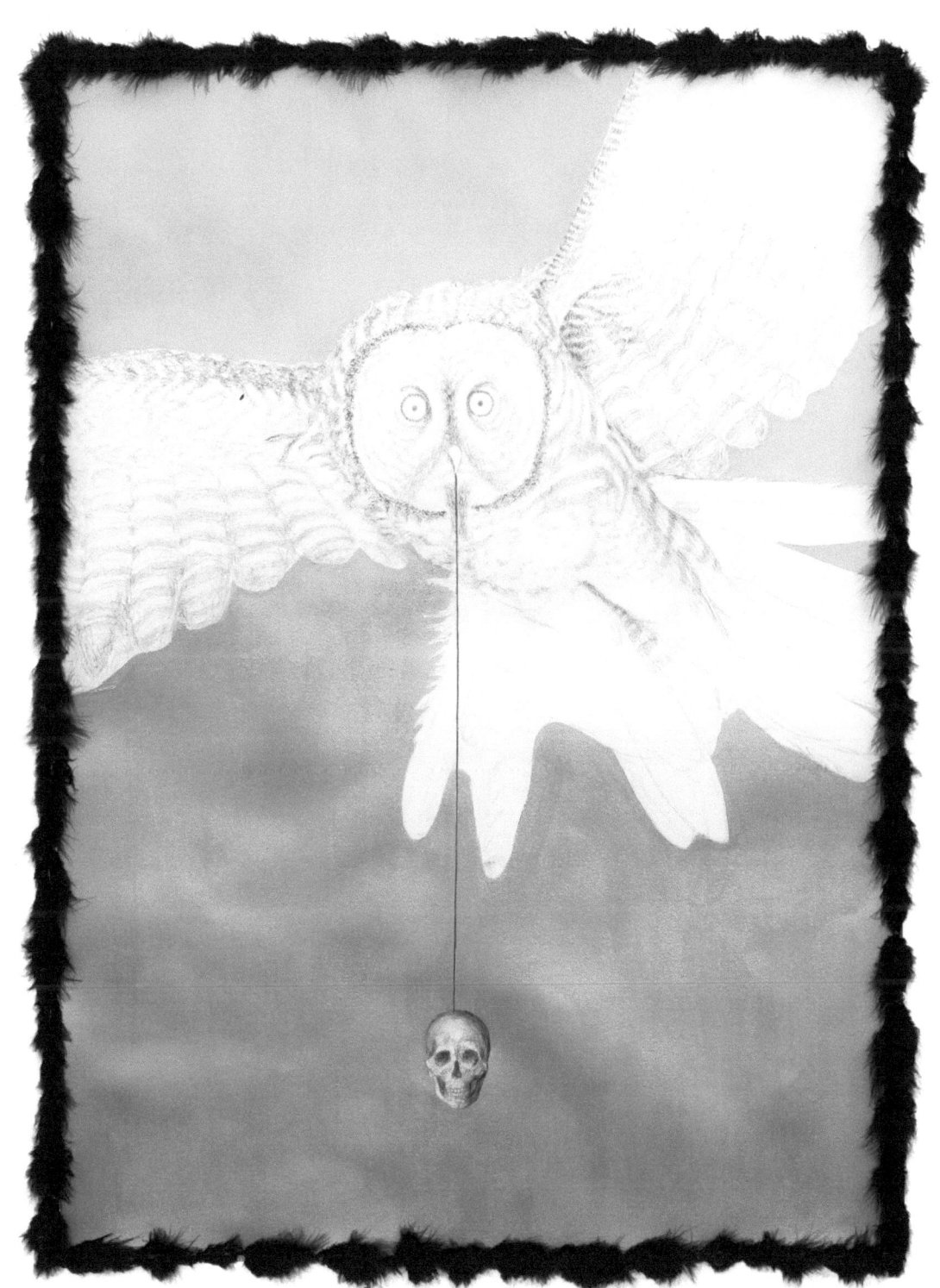

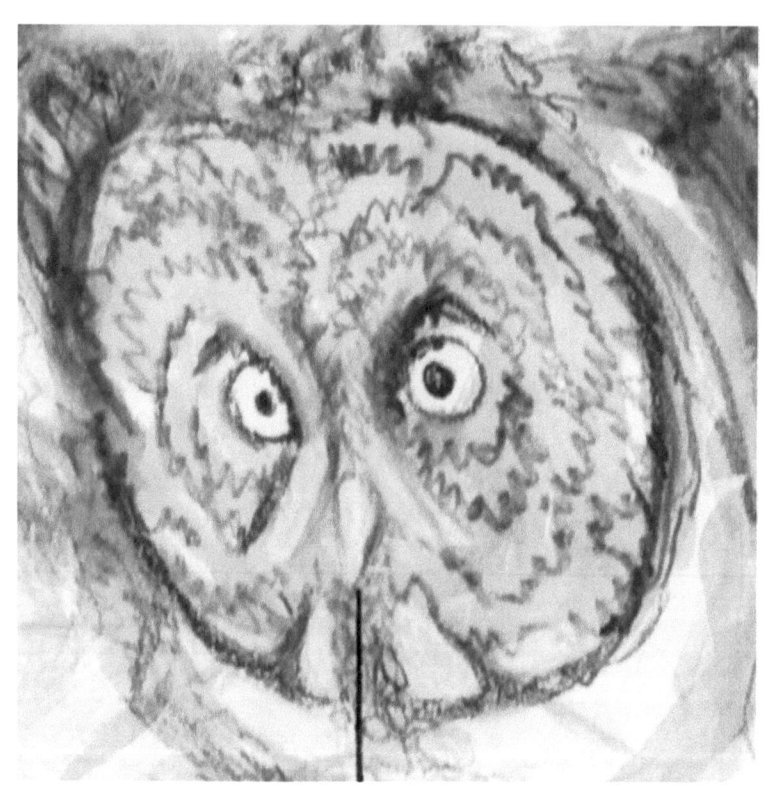

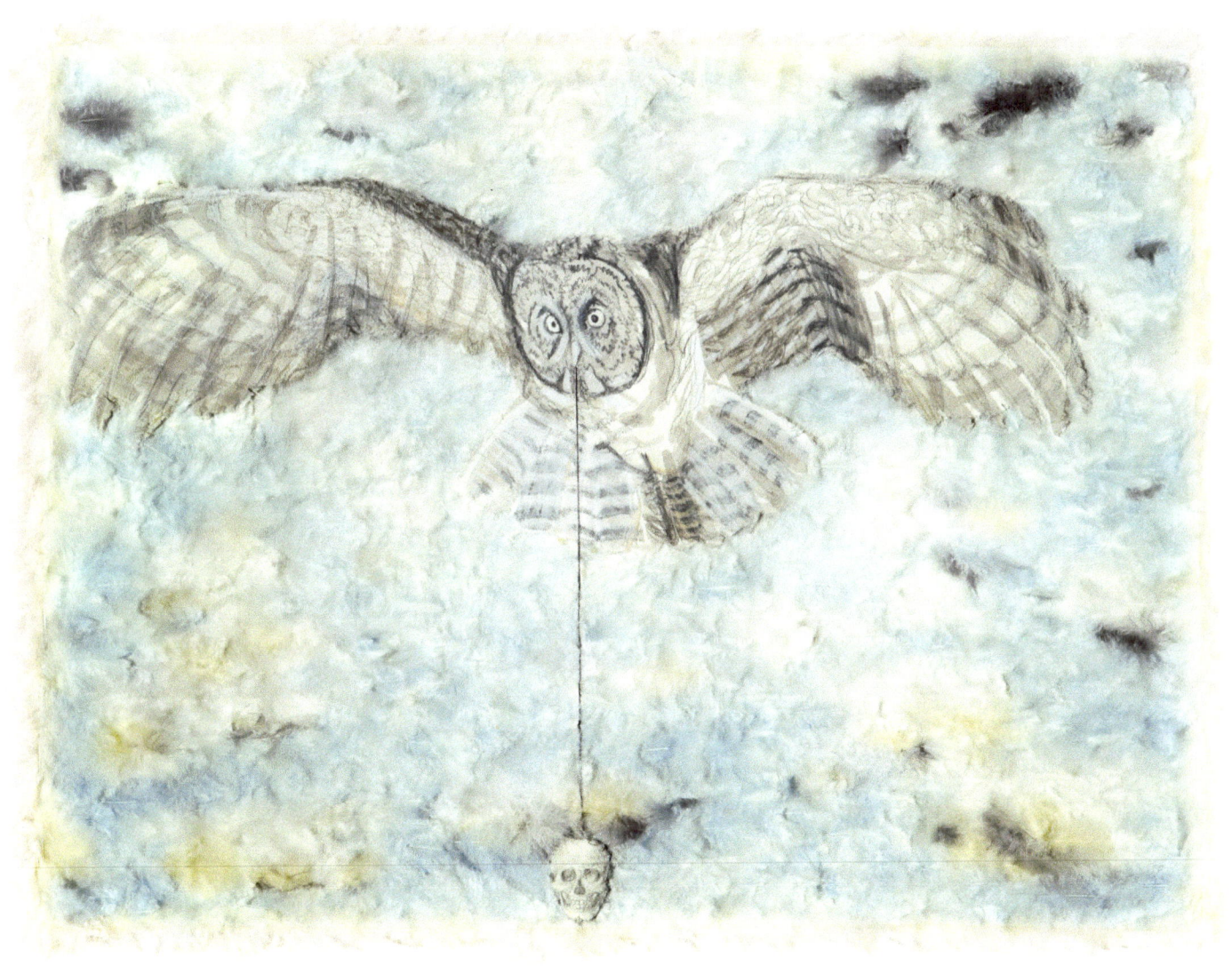

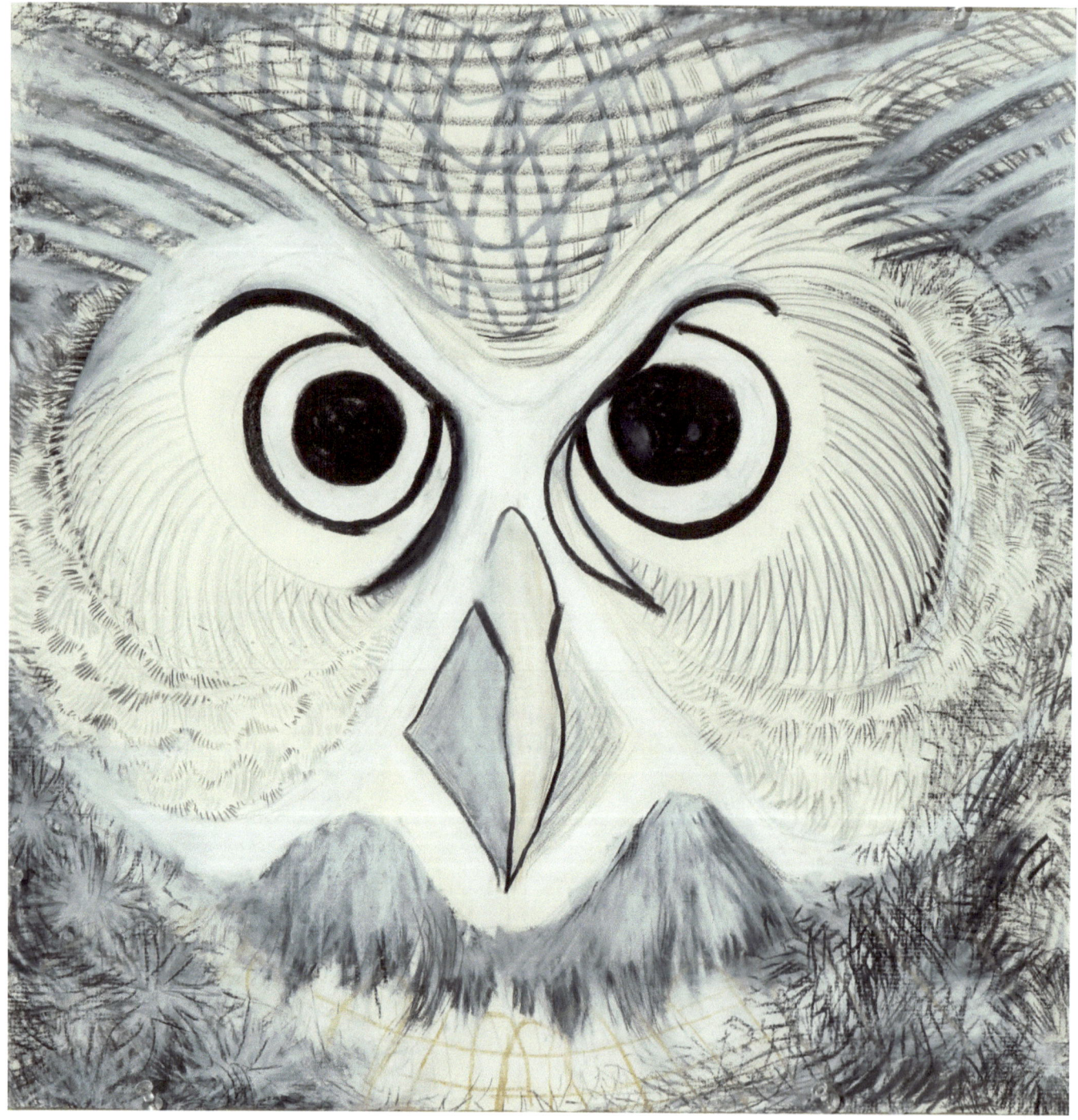

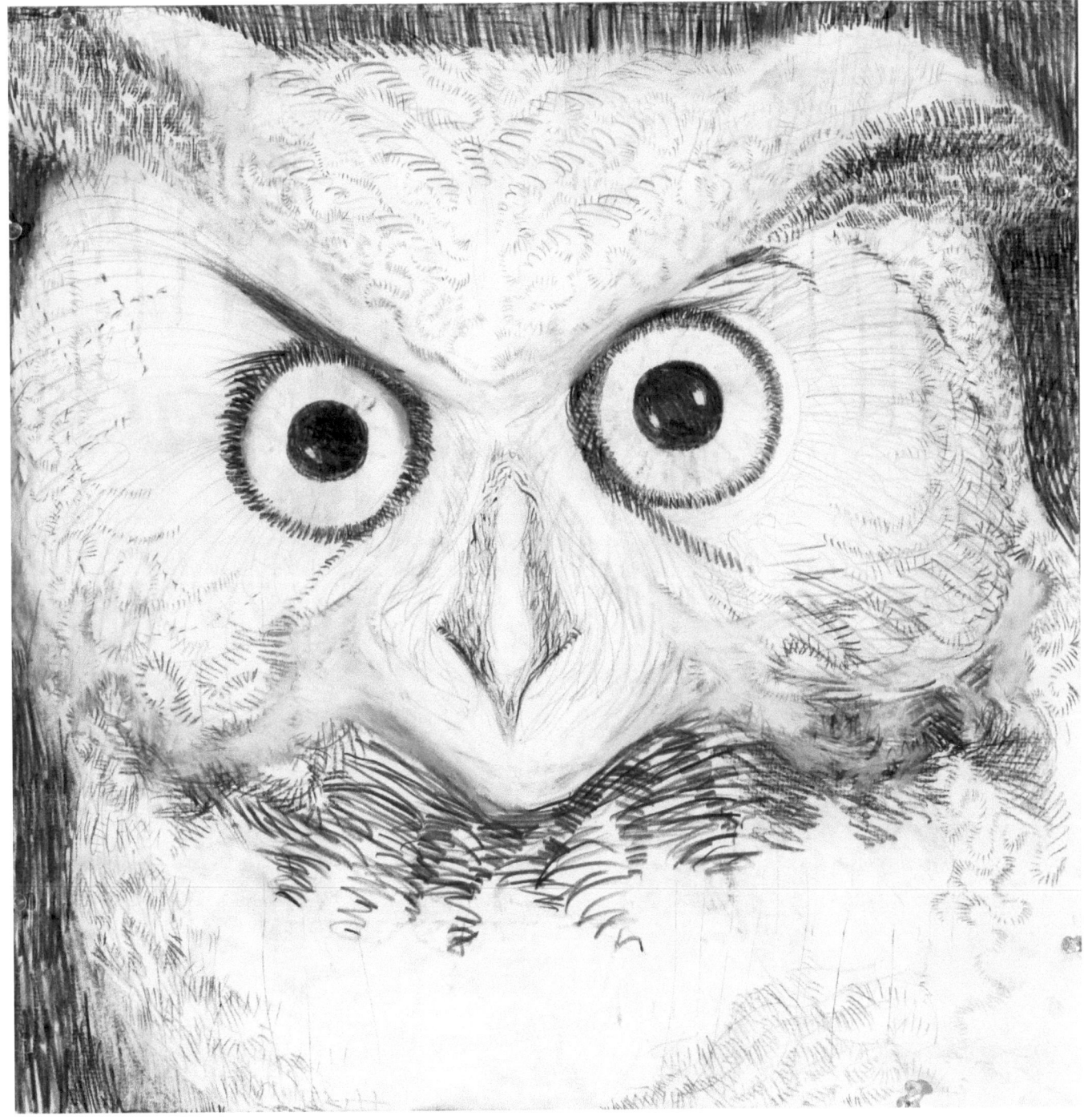

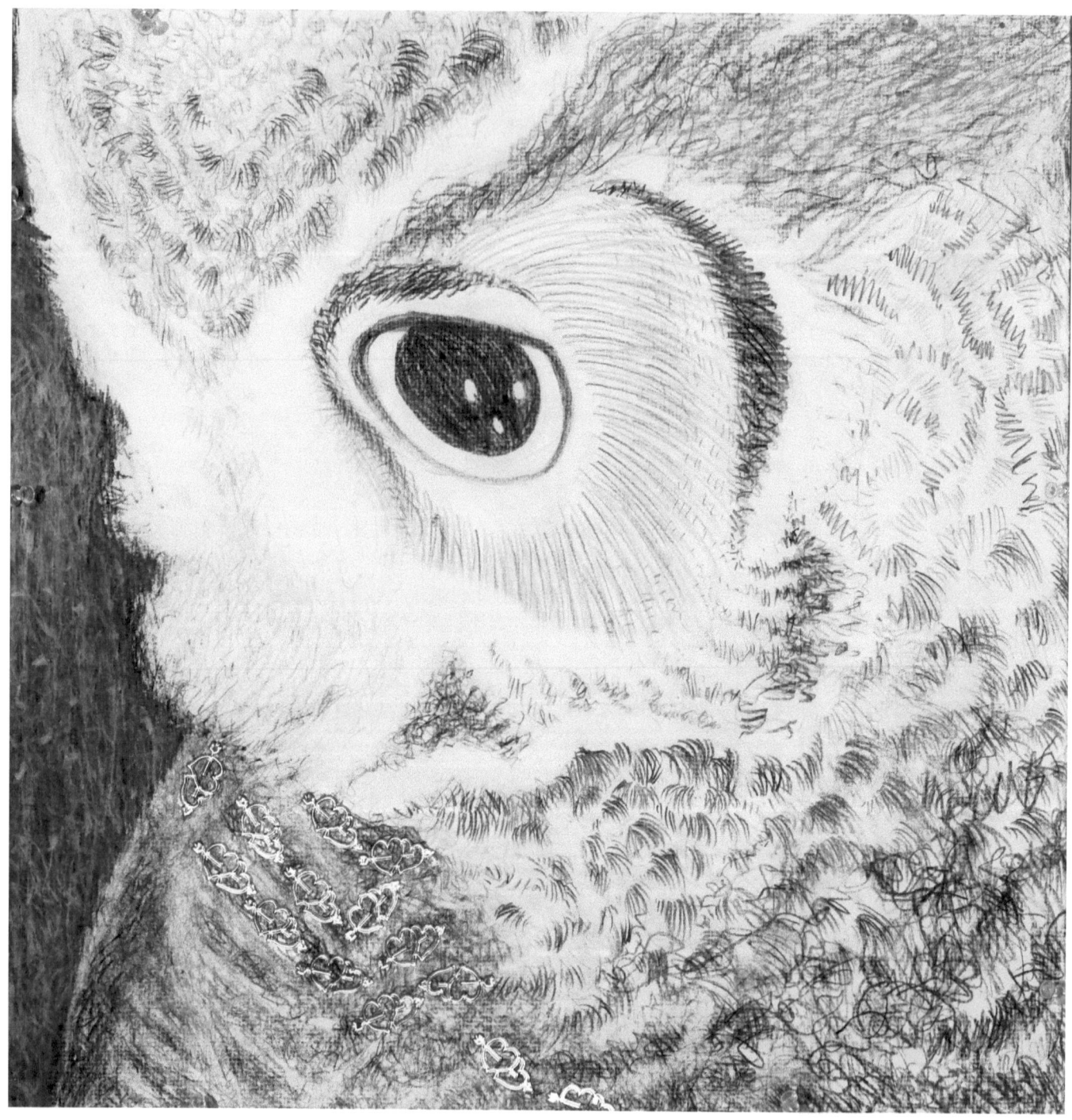

41

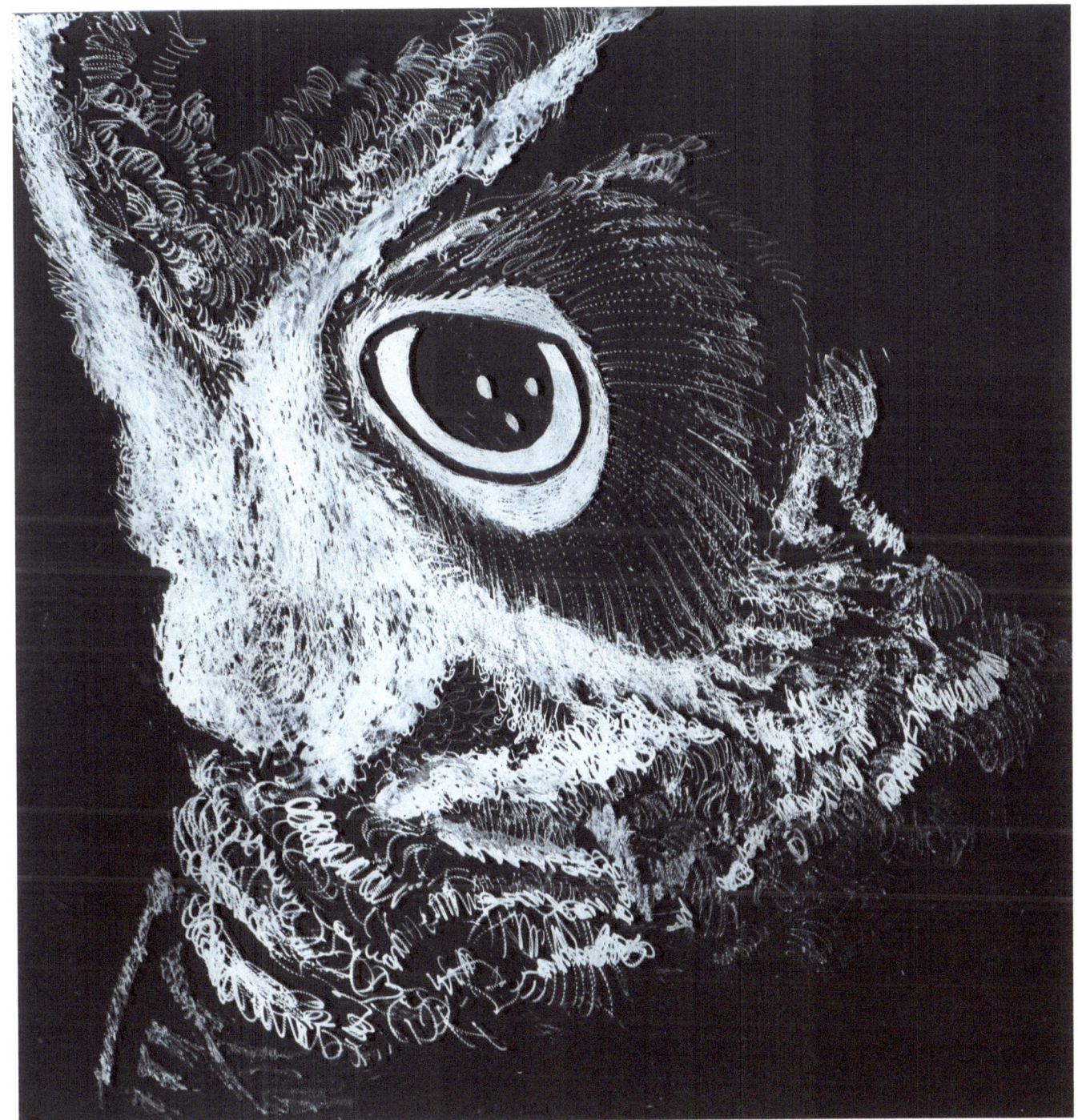

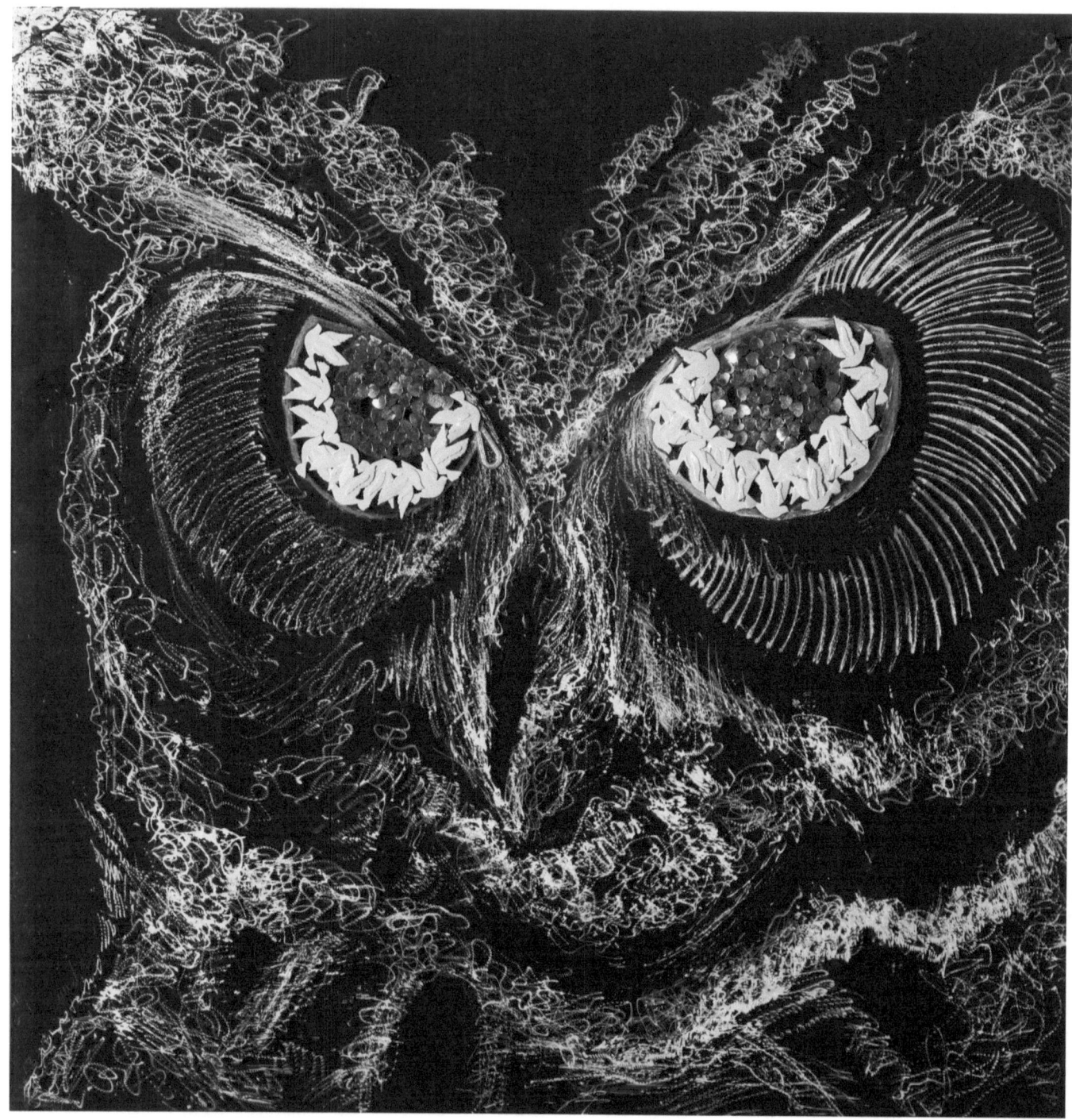

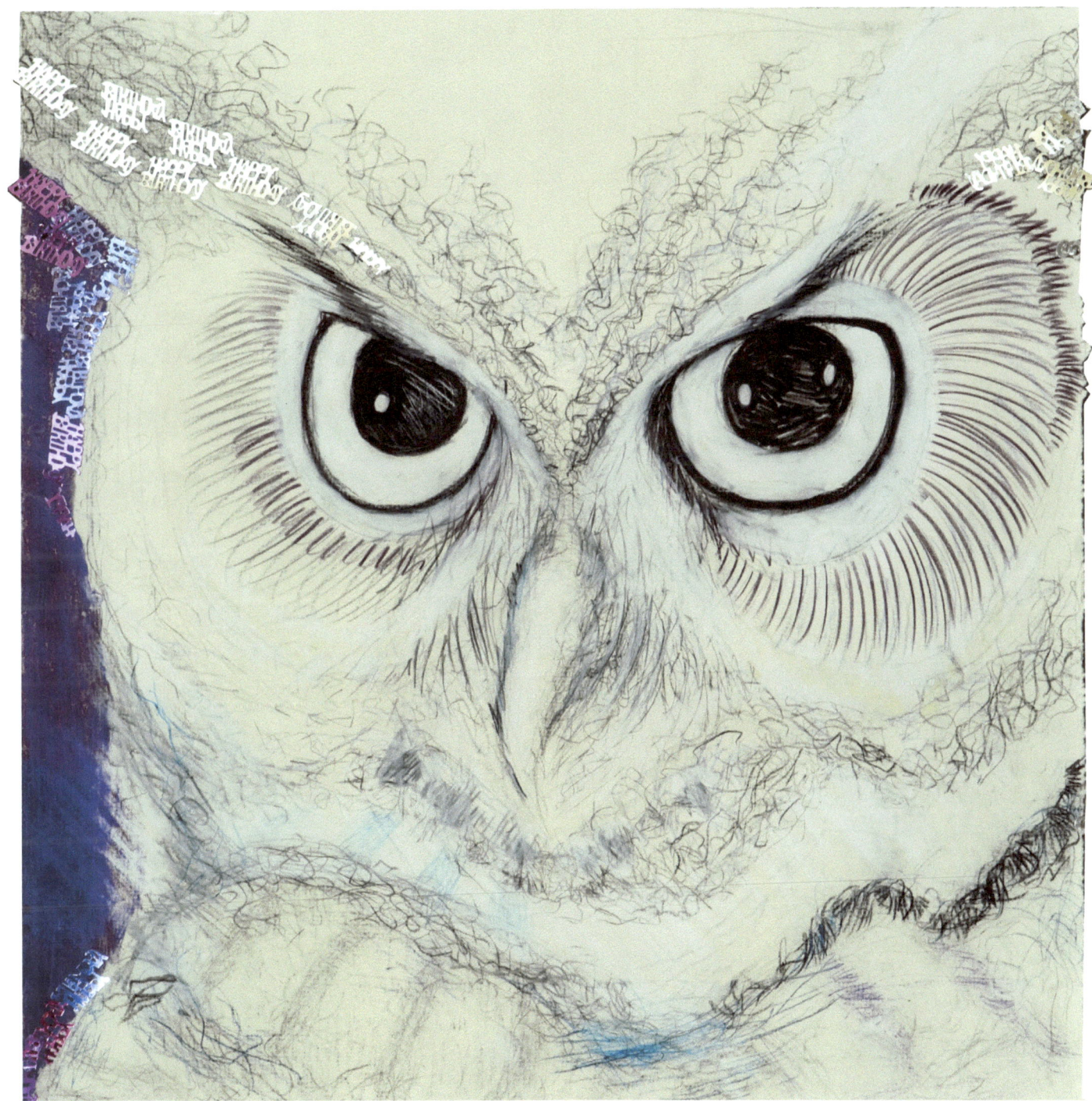

44

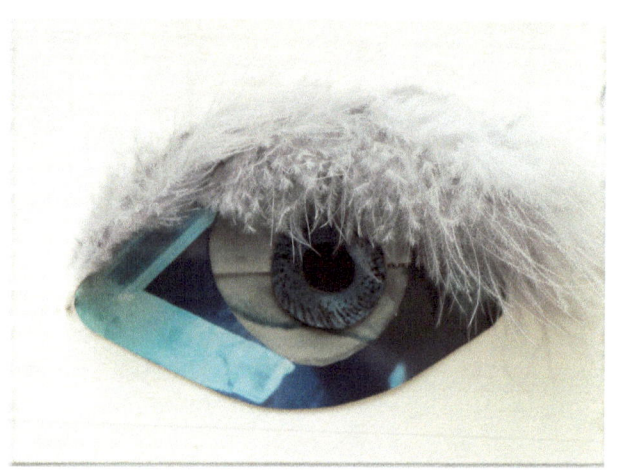

Working in series of related imagery allows me to sequentially explore ideas and materials. This group of images examines the bond/rupture between human and animal nature. I am interested in the extent and balance of these natures expressed in interaction with our environment. Many questions are posited. Are helicopters and birds related? Can technical ingenuity and awe of flight connect us to our animal heritage? Is it our nature to create and destroy? I am concerned with the role of time in answering these questions.

In each image a contained narrative world is defined and also distorted. This is a world where birds play a spiritual and psychological role usually assigned to humans. The space in each is a reflection of the familiar three-dimensional world we are trained to read from two-dimensional information. Here the edges of the picture plane have been bowed-out, or interrupted, warping the space slightly, creating a sense of ill-ease. The images suggest a debasement of the environment, a possible consequence of violence or a cycle of destruction not typical - animals apparently triumphant over (or unaffected by) the humans whose skulls they carry off. There are hopeful passages - an egg in a nest, new growth of colorful trees, a glimpse of the future.

In the diptych, Song of Icarus, a drawing with collage elements, the exchange of human and animal characteristics is manifest in the use of feathers for the woman's hair and human hair for the falling bird. The fact that there are literally two halves to the work is a reflection of this duality. The world seems orderly yet contains bizarre events: helicopters carried off by a giant bird, or taking off from the rib cage of the woman. A bird falls into the sea. A cloud of uncertain composition abuts a dotted and barred sky. An underlying structure of receding rectangles creates a grid suggesting pages of a sketchbook; perception through the passage of time.

I envision a three-dimensional component to this series which would be site specific. In it there would be life-size (meaning the size in the images) cut-outs of many of the birds and their cargo which would hang from the ceiling near the wall-mounted drawings and mixed-media works.

images

p. 1   Owl Drooling Plastic   9" x 8 ½"
        Caran d'Ache neocolor crayon, pencil, plastic party contetti on paper.

p. 3   Dark Passage #3   18" x 18"
        Intaglio ink, Caran d'Ache neocolor crayon, pencil on paper.

p. 4   Dark Passage #6   18" x 18"
        Intaglio ink, Caran d'Ache neocolor crayon, crushed glass,
        water-based paint on paper.

p. 5   Dark Passage #7   18 ¾" x 18 ½"
        Intaglio ink, vintage embroidered cashmere fabric,
        Caran d'Ache neocolor crayon on paper.

p. 6   Dark Passage #8   21" x 19"
        Intaglio ink, Caran d'Ache neocolor crayon, Stabilo Woody,
        cut and folded paper on paper.

p. 7   Dark Passage #1   18" x 18"
        Intaglio ink, Caran d'Ache neocolor crayon on paper.

p. 8   Dark Passage #4   18" x 18"
        Intaglio ink, Caran d'Ache neocolor crayon, collaged etching on paper.

p. 9   Red Sky   18" x 18 ½"
        Intaglio ink, Caran d'Ache neocolor crayon, Stabilo Woody on paper.

p. 10   Blighted Summer   18" x 18 ½"
        Intaglio ink, Caran d'Ache neocolor crayon, vintage needlepoint on paper.

p. 11   Dark Passage #5   18" x 18"
        Intaglio ink, Caran d'Ache neocolor crayon, turkey feathers,
        pencil on paper.

p. 12   Swimming with Kafka   18 ½" x 18"
        Intaglio ink, Caran d'Ache neocolor crayon, water-based paint on paper.

p. 13   Jack in the Box   32" x 25"
        Pencil, vintage embroidered cashmere fabric, slides, water-based paint,
        paper collage elements on acrylic sheet.

p. 14   Hope   28 ¼" x 28"
         Intaglio ink, Caran d'Ache neocolor crayon, pencil, paper and
         photo collage elements on acrylic sheet.

p. 15   Mad Dog   18" x 23"
         Intaglio ink, Caran d'Ache neocolor crayon, water-based paint,
         pencil on paper.

p. 16   Masquerade   20" x 21"
         Intaglio ink, Caran d'Ache neocolor crayon on paper.

p. 17   Squadron   18 ½" x 18"
         Intaglio ink, Caran d'Ache neocolor crayon, vintage needlepoint
         on paper.

p. 18   Crash   18 ½" x 18"
         Intaglio ink, crushed glass, sequins, Caran d'Ache neocolor crayon
         on paper.

p. 19   Omen   20" x 20"
Intaglio ink, Caran d'Ache neocolor crayon, pencil, water-based paint,
Stabilo Woody on paper.

p. 20   Pink Helicopter   24" x 20 ½"
Intaglio ink, vintage needlepoint, Caran d'Ache neocolor crayon,
Stabilo Woody, pencil on paper.

p. 21   Song of Icarus (left side of diptych)   48" x 36"
Caran d'Ache neocolor crayon, Stabilo Woody, color pencil, water-based
paint, feathers, vintage needlepoint, human hair on paper.

p. 22   Song of Icarus (right side of diptych)   48" x 36"
Caran d'Ache neocolor crayon, Stabilo Woody, color pencil, vintage
needlepoint on paper.

p. 23   Journey   22" x 30"
Turkey feathers, Caran d'Ache neocolor crayon on paper.

| p. 24 | Hanged Man | 22" x 30" |
| | Pencil, turkey feathers on paper. | |

| p. 25 | Hanged Man #2 | 22" x 30" |
| | Ink, Caran d'Ache neocolor crayon, water-based paint, marker, paper collage element on denril. | |

| p. 26 | Hanged Man #3 | 22 ½" x 30 ½" |
| | Ink, Caran d'Ache neocolor crayon, pencil, turkey feathers on denril. | |

| p. 27 | Spring | 31½" x 42" |
| | Ink, vintage textiles, turkey feathers, water-based paint on paper. | |

| p. 28 | Offering | 31 ½" x 42" |
| | Vintage textiles, Caran d'Ache neocolor crayon, water-based paint, Stabilo Woody, pencil on paper. | |

| p. 29 - 30 | Return (and detail) | 31 ½" x 42" |
| | Vintage textiles, tulle, Caran d'Ache neocolor crayon, Stabilo Woody, water-based paint, sequins, beaded fabric on paper. | |

p. 31 - 32   Crown of Thorns (and detail)   30" x 22"
Lithography ink, water-based paint, paper and denril collage elements, beaded fabric on paper.

p. 33 - 34   Cat's Cradle (and detail)   32 ½" x 21 ½"
Water-based paint, turkey feathers on paper.

p. 35 - 36   Silver Owl (and detail)   42 ½" x 32
Water-based paint, turkey feathers, pencil on paper.

p. 37 - 38   Feathered Sky (and detail)   32 ½" x 42 ½"
Turkey feathers, water-based paint on paper.

p. 39   Owl Headshot #1   18" x 18"
Caran d'Ache neocolor crayon, pencil on paper.

p. 40   Owl Headshot #2   18" x 18"
Pencil, Caran d'Ache neocolor crayon on paper.

p. 41   Owl Headshot #3   18" x 18"
         Pencil, Caran d'Ache neocolor crayon, plastic party confetti on paper.

p. 42   Dark Owl Headshot #3   18" x 18"
         Acrylic paint on incised acrylic sheet.

p. 43   Dark Owl Headshot #4   18" x 18"
         Acrylic paint, plastic party confetti on incised acrylic sheet.

p. 44   Owl Headshot #4   18"x 18"
         Pencil, Caran d'Ache neocolor crayon, plastic party confetti on paper.

p. 45   Feathered Eye   2" x 3"
         Feather, photographic transparency, photograph.

front cover   detail of Cat's Cradle, page 34
back cover   detail of Silver Owl, page 36

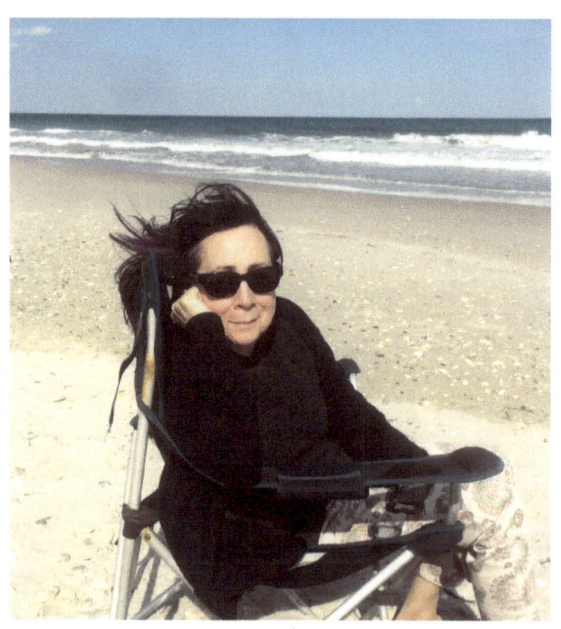

photograph by Catherine Nesbit

MARGARET WEBER AND DRAWING ROOMS
by James Pustorino, Victory Hall Executive Director

Margaret Weber is known as artist, teacher, curator and arts and community organizer in Jersey City. Margaret was always a valuable supporter and friend of Victory Hall when we were a busy community cultural center throughout the early 2000s. In 2012, her long time devotion to enriching city life led her to work with Victory Hall as we re-shaped ourselves as an arts organization and arts center that could engage artists and the public from New Jersey and the New York City metropolitan area. The new arts center we launched later that year, the Drawing Rooms, encountered many challenges, from the immediate - as Hurricane Sandy engulfed our building during our first month - to long term issues of sustainability and artistic and economic development. As Chair of the Steering Committee, Margaret provided both the direction and strength that allowed us to re-open our Center seven months after Sandy. We continue to succeed in overcoming the obstacles before us. As one of the arts professionals who settled in Jersey City and formed an arts community in the past few decades, Margaret has helped us become who we are as an organization through sharing her artwork, ideas, experiences and resolve.

Victory Hall Press was started in 2010 with the purpose of furthering the work of area artists. Gathering and presenting their artwork in a book format amplifies their ideas and allows us to keep part of that artist as a person with us. It is wonderful for us to be able to present this edition of Margaret Weber's "Birds of Pray" and make her artwork, which is so filled with her thoughts and expressive of her internal visions, easily available to a wider public. Thanks to Emily de Rham who worked on this production and thanks to Margaret for sharing so much with us.